Every Believer's Authority

Over All the Power of the Enemy

Every Believer's Authority

Over All the Power of the Enemy

Rev. Bill Ferg

© Copyright 1995 — Rev. Bill Ferg

All rights reserved. This book is protected under the copyright laws of the United States of America. This book may not be copied or reprinted for commercial gain or profit. The use of short quotations or occasional page copying for personal or group study is permitted and encouraged. Permission will be granted upon request. Unless otherwise identified, Scripture quotations are from the New King James Version. Copyright ©1979, 1980, 1982, Thomas Nelson, Inc. Scripture quotations marked (AMP) are taken from The Amplified Bible, Old Testament. Copyright © 1965, 1987 by The Zondervan Corporation. The Amplified New Testament, copyright ©1954, 1958, 1987 by The Lockman Foundation. Used by permission.

Take note that the name satan and related names are not capitalized. We choose not to acknowledge him, even to the point of violating grammatical rules.

Treasure House
An Imprint of
Destiny Image
P.O. Box 310
Shippensburg, PA 17257-0310
"For where your treasure is
there will your heart be also." Matthew 6:21

ISBN 1-56043-843-6

For Worldwide Distribution
Printed in the U.S.A.

Treasure House books are available through these fine distributors outside the United States:

Christian Growth, Inc.	Vine Christian Centre
Jalan Kilang-Timor, Singapore 0315	Mid Glamorgan, Wales, United Kingdom
Rhema Ministries Trading	Vision Resources
Randburg, South Africa	Ponsonby, Auckland, New Zealand
Salvation Book Centre	WA Buchanan Company
Petaling, Jaya, Malaysia	Geebung, Queensland, Australia
Successful Christian Living	Word Alive
Capetown, Rep. of South Africa	Niverville, Manitoba, Canada

Inside the U.S., call toll free to order:
1-800-722-6774

Dedication

I dedicate this book to my wife, Dawn, and to our children. I thank God for their love and patience with me.

I also thank Sally Fox for all her hard work and dedication to this project.

Contents

	Foreword	ix
	Introduction	xi
Chapter 1	Lord, I'll Believe in Miracles	1
Chapter 2	Every Believer's Authority	13
Chapter 3	Our Authority Comes From Heaven	37
Chapter 4	Exercise Your Authority With Humility and Boldness	55
Chapter 5	God's Word Gives Us Authority for Healing	71
Chapter 6	Don't Put God in a Box	85

Foreword

I consider it a privilege to introduce you to this excellent book, *Every Believer's Authority*. My recommendation is, of course, based on the content of the message, but also on the character of the author.

I know Bill Ferg as a godly man who spends time with the Father, getting to know Him, communicating with Him, and hearing Him. He is a man who has studied to show himself approved unto God, "rightly dividing the word of truth" (2 Tim. 2:15).

He has taken the truths he has learned and appropriately applied them to the ministry the Lord has entrusted to him.

The testimonies, especially that of baby Saul, will touch your heart as you recognize that this man lives what he preaches. He makes no apologies for his bold faith, and teaches us all of *Every Believer's Authority*.

Dave Esala
Founder/President
Herald International Missions, Inc.

Introduction

I pray that as you read *Every Believer's Authority* you will learn the same truths that I have discovered through the Holy Spirit since I became a born-again Christian. As you read the pages of this book, don't skip past the Scriptures "to get to the good parts." God's word *is* the good part, and those passages will bring light and power to the things I share with you about your authority in Christ.

Before I was saved, satan had his way with me. But when I asked Jesus Christ to save me and deliver me from sin and temptation, He did. Now it is my turn to help others.

"Therefore, if anyone is in Christ, he is a new creation; old things have passed away; behold, all things have become new" (2 Cor. 5:17). When I began my new life in Christ Jesus, I needed to learn what my position was as a child of God.

But you are a chosen generation, a royal priesthood, a holy nation, His own special people, that you may proclaim the praises of Him who called you out of darkness into His marvelous light; who once were not a people but are now the people of God, who had not obtained mercy but now have obtained mercy (1 Peter 2:9-10).

Behold, I give you the authority to trample on serpents and scorpions, and over all the power of the enemy, and nothing shall by any means hurt you (Luke 10:19).

Pray and ask the Holy Spirit to reveal the truth of His Word to you.

But God, who is rich in mercy, because of His great love with which He loved us, even when we were dead in trespasses, made us alive together with Christ (by grace you have been saved), and raised us up together, and made us sit together in the heavenly places in Christ Jesus, that in the ages to come He might show the exceeding riches of His grace in His kindness toward us in Christ Jesus. For by grace you have been saved through faith, and that not of yourselves; it is the gift of God, not of works, lest anyone should boast. For we are His workmanship, created in Christ Jesus for good works, which God prepared beforehand that we should walk in them (Ephesians 2:4-10).

Several years ago I joined Denny Nisley, the street preacher, in New Orleans to preach the gospel to sinners at the annual Mardi Gras celebration. Each day and into the night, we invaded the old French Quarter of New Orleans around the Bourbon Street area. There is never any shortage of sinners down there. Every vile and degrading thing that satan has dreamed up can be found there—homosexuality, transvestism, prostitution, pedophilia, drug addiction, alcoholism, and the like. It is a cesspool of hurt, pain, and hopelessness.

My desire has always been to show the people the love of Jesus, the one who set me free and who died for them also. On one of these nights a group of us were preaching in front of a homosexual bar on Bourbon Street. The place was so packed with homosexual men that they were overflowing out into the sidewalk and street. One of the people with me was preaching a burning message to these people telling them that there was a better life and they didn't have to live this way, and that Jesus Christ was the answer.

Did you know that every homosexual has one great desire? They all want to be straight, but apart from the miraculous of the power of Jesus Christ they are bound to satan's lies and cannot get free. Homosexuality is a spirit sent from satan. People aren't born homosexual; they accept satan's temptation through molestation and abuse or by their own free will. Jesus is the deliverer and He is more than able to set sinners free—even the homosexual.

As the Word was being preached, the homosexuals became convicted. However, rather than repent, they got angry with us and came out into the street where we were and started a riot. They threw rocks at us, along with beer cans, chunks of wood, trash, and anything else they could get their hands on. In just a few minutes, the police came along to break it up. In the midst of the riot, though, someone grabbed my arm and asked me to help a man sitting on a step in front of a building across the street from the bar.

I approached the man and asked if he needed help. As I did, he began to foam at the mouth and his eyes rolled back in their sockets. His face became distorted and he looked like a different person. His whole body began to slither up the wooden door he was leaning against—but he wasn't pushing himself up, he was levitating. His legs were outstretched and limp in front of him. As he slid up the door, the flesh on his back was scraped raw and torn. He had no control over what was happening to him because the devil was in control of his entire being. His head began to bounce on the door like a basketball bouncing on a gym floor. Eight or ten times it bounced back and forth, each time making a horrible thud sound... thud, thud, thud, thud, thud, thud, thud, thud, thud. (You can read a similar account in Luke 9:38-39.) Finally the abuse ended, and the man collapsed on the sidewalk and begged us, "Please help me. They're coming again to get me." The demons were coming back.

Two other homosexual men had followed this man out of the bar because they wanted to take him and abuse him some more, but I stood between this man and them and told them to "take a hike." They still insisted that this man was with them. As I was confronting the two men, a police officer walked over and asked what was going on.

By the Spirit of God, I asked the officer, "Have you ever seen demons manifesting?" He said, "No." I replied, "Then this doesn't concern you, officer. You should probably leave because we are going to cast these demons out of this man!" When he heard that, the police officer said, "Okay," and quickly turned and walked away into the night.

The three believers who were standing there with me helped me pick up the demon-possessed man and carry him to a safe place to get him set free. As we helped him down the street, the man went from a conscious state a nearly unconscious state as the demons tormented him without mercy. At one point we had to pass a bar. We were three blocks away when the man started screaming because he saw demons hanging around the bar, and some of them were homosexual spirits.

We changed course to a different direction, but right after that the demons manifested again. This time they threw the man to the ground and thrashed him around until he was cut and bleeding. Two of us tried to restrain the man so he wouldn't hurt himself, but he had such supernatural strength that he tossed us around so much we couldn't hold him!

After this, we took the man to a park where we met some other Christians from our group. Over the next hour, we cast demons out of him. At one point he levitated eight inches off the ground again, like he did when we first found him leaning against the wooden door. We had him denounce homosexuality and plead the Blood of Jesus. This man had been a born-again, Spirit-filled Christian who had been a homosexual before he was saved. He was on his way to a Bible school in Florida, and was passing through New Orleans when his bus had a layover. At this point he yielded to the temptation to visit the French Quarter, and when he did, he yielded to a second temptation, to visit a homosexual bar. Like many Christians today, he thought he was able to overcome any temptation (although he had just yielded to two big ones).

Let me tell you plainly and clearly: Don't ever mess with sin. The Bible says we are to resist the devil (see Jas. 4:7). We have authority in Christ Jesus, but we can't act foolishly. We must avoid all appearances of evil (see 1 Thess. 5:22). If you play with fire, you will get burnt. After this man entered the homosexual bar, he was approached by other homosexuals and they just used and abused him.

He felt such shame and remorse that he decided to end his life that night. He didn't think God could ever forgive him again, and he hated himself. But then his heart was moved one last time when he heard the preaching in the street, and he knew if he could only get to us, we would be able to help him. By the time he managed to reach the street where we were, he had been totally overtaken by a multitude of demons.

When an unclean spirit goes out of a man, he goes through dry places, seeking rest; and finding none, he says, "I will return to my house from which I came." And when he comes, he finds it swept and put in order. Then he goes and takes with him seven other spirits more wicked than himself, and they enter and dwell there; and the last state of that man is worse than the first (Luke 11:24-26).

Praise God, that man was set free that night by the power of Jesus Christ. He went to Teen Challenge and is living for the Lord today, free from homosexuality! He still writes to me and thanks me for being there for him that night. Had I not known my authority in Christ, he wouldn't have been set free. He would have died a homosexual, maybe even that night!

I hope you enjoy reading *Every Believer's Authority* as much as I have enjoyed writing it.

God bless you.

In Christ Jesus,
Bill Ferg

Chapter 1

Lord, I'll Believe in Miracles

I remember it as though it were yesterday. I was 11 years old, and sitting in the weekly Sunday school class with about a dozen other children.

The Sunday school teacher had just finished teaching us a Bible story where Jesus healed a blind man, and one of the students asked, "Why don't we still see miracles today?"

With a smile on his face and a little chuckle, this so-called man of God and teacher of the Word explained to the whole class, "The day of miracles has passed. We don't need miracles anymore because we now have technology and modern medicine."

Maybe I was only an 11-year-old boy, but I didn't accept that. I didn't argue because who was I? I was just a little kid. But right there in that classroom, I silently prayed this little prayer: "Dear Lord Jesus, I don't know if the things our Sunday school teacher is saying are right, but I know this, Jesus: If You ever want to show me a miracle, I will believe it. Amen."

Every Believer's Authority

I just prayed a simple little prayer of faith and God heard me. At 15 years of age, I received the call of God on my life, but I didn't obey. Instead I lived contrary to God's Word for many years. But at the age of 31, I called out to God to save me and He did. The call of God was still there waiting for me, and miracles have been a part of my life and ministry ever since then.

How I Learned About Healing

Shortly after my wife and I received Jesus Christ as Lord and Savior, we had to face the pain and heartbreak of our son's terrible ear condition.

Ever since Adam was born, he had suffered from continuous and painful ear infections. The doctors told us his eardrums and inner ears were not properly formed at birth, and this caused infections to settle in his ears. The pain almost drove our son mad. Adam would only have one or two good days out of a week, and the rest of the time he suffered in unbearable pain.

We took Adam to every "ear, nose, and throat specialist" we could find. We had tubes put in; we tried new experimental drugs; but none of these treatments had any real effect.

By the time Adam was three-and-a-half years old, the doctors told us he couldn't take much more of the medications. They were afraid the drugs would damage his kidneys, or even worse, even cause them to shut down.

When we heard this news, Dawn and I lost our last ray of hope. We didn't know what to do next. That evening, as a new believer, I decided to pray and ask the Lord to lead us to a good doctor who could treat our son. I felt there had to be a doctor somewhere who could help our son.

That evening, after everyone had gone to bed, I sat on the sofa and began to ask the Lord to lead me to the "right doctor." As I prayed, I heard an inner voice in my spirit say to me, "Go to your son and cup your hands around his head. Place a finger in each ear and pray for him."

Now, I had been a Christian for only five months at that time, and I had heard little or nothing about healing (except what my Sunday school teacher said 20 years before). My wife and I had just come out of a denominational church where there was no teaching. This was all foreign and strange to me.

Hearing from the Holy Spirit was also very new, but I believed I had heard something that wasn't from me. I knew enough to know that it wasn't the devil because I was "born again" and serving Jesus Christ. I knew that when you serve Him, the devil has no right to you. I knew that if we ask the Lord for something good, He will not allow us to receive something evil. "How much more will your Father who is in heaven give good things to those who ask Him!" (Mt. 7:11b)

I decided I would act on this word that I had received, so I went into my son's room and sat on the edge of the bed. I woke Adam up and told him I was

Every Believer's Authority

going to pray for his ears, and that God was going to heal him. I did it exactly as I had heard it in my spirit. I cupped his head in my hands and placed the middle finger of each hand in his ears—just as I had heard it—and prayed for my son's ears to be healed. It took less than 45 seconds. Then my little boy said, "Thank you, Dad," rolled over, and went to sleep.

The next day, my son was in very good spirits and had no pain. In fact, for the next four months, Adam took no medication. He saw no doctors, and he had no ear infections or pain whatsoever.

Now, I had not told my wife or anyone else about hearing from the Holy Spirit, or about praying for our son. I just wasn't sure if she would understand, for we had both heard people laugh at ministers who prayed for the sick and heard them called names. So I just kept this to myself and pondered it.

After four months, it was time for Adam's yearly check-up. When Dawn and Adam came home from the doctor's appointment that day, Dawn was extremely excited and full of joy. She told me that something awesome had happened to our son's ears. She said that when the doctor began to shine his lighted instrument into Adam's ears, he repeatedly went back and forth from one ear to the other, and then he checked his records several times.

Finally, with a puzzled look on his face, he said to my wife, "Is this *the same Adam Ferg* we have been treating for ear infections?"

"Well, yes. Why do you ask?"

"How long has it been since he had any ear aches?" he asked.

Dawn thought for a moment and realized it had been several months since he had been sick.

The doctor finally shook his head and said, "This is incredible! I remember Adam's ear problems. I even remember writing in his records that both eardrums are a mass of scars, and they look like raw hamburger. I even diagnosed him with a 30-percent hearing loss! But today, Adam's ears are perfect. In fact, there is no sign that they were ever infected." The doctor even said *the tubes he had surgically inserted in Adam's ears a year before were gone.* His ears were new!

When Dawn was finished, I told her what had happened and how I prayed for Adam. I took our son to the best doctor you will ever find. His name is Jesus.

It is interesting that when people start talking about how God is sovereign, most of them want to explain why some people aren't healed by God. "Maybe He won't heal you because it is not His plan. *He is sovereign, after all.* He will decide what He will do, and He will decide who He will heal, *because God is a sovereign God.*"

Do you know what? God's Word is sovereign and, unlike man, He doesn't go against His Word. His Word is already settled in Heaven and on earth (see Ps. 119:89). So when somebody says God is sovereign, our reaction should be "Praise God, then that person should get healed; that person should be delivered from mental torment and anguish; for God's

Every Believer's Authority

Word has been settled in Heaven." According to God's Word, everyone can be healed.

The Word says that God's law is spiritual, and it will heal the flesh (see Rom. 7:14). It will deliver us. It is sovereign. It is simple. God's Word is sovereign, just as He is, and He acts according to His Word. God will not act apart from His Word. His Word is a direct insight into God's nature. We make a promise and say, "Yes, I'll do this or I'll do that." But when the time comes to do the thing we promised, we say, "Sorry, it is not convenient for me."

When does God ever say that something is not convenient for Him? He is not like man. He doesn't operate in our mental capacity. He is far, far above that. He is on a higher level, a perfect level. When God says something, that's it. It's settled. It doesn't change. You can rest on it. You can trust it. You can rely on it forever and ever. It is good in every situation.

Therefore, when you hear somebody talking about the sovereignty of God, you say, "Yes, His Word is sovereign and it can't be changed. His Word says that we are healed by His stripes. The Word says that He sent His Word and healed us" (see 1 Pet. 2:24; Ps. 107:20). It is sovereign.

Doesn't that make it clear? God's Word is so simple, but you know, most people try to explain it away or change it. They do their best to make God's Word "fit in" with their thinking, or support some doctrine or teaching that they have picked up along the way or

6

Lord, I'll Believe in Miracles

from their church. What we need to do is get ahold of God's Word and see what God says, then *believe it*.

But as it is written: "Eye has not seen, nor ear heard, nor have entered into the heart of man the things which God has prepared for those who love Him." But God has revealed them to us through His Spirit. For the Spirit searches all things, yes, the deep things of God. For what man knows the things of a man except the spirit of the man which is in him? Even so no one knows the things of God except the Spirit of God. Now we have received, not the spirit of the world, but the Spirit who is from God, that we might know the things that have been freely given to us by God (1 Corinthians 2:9-12).

Do you see how many times the apostle Paul speaks of the Spirit there? He doesn't say, "Well, it is the mind of man that understands." In fact, he says, "Eye has not seen, nor ear heard" the things of God that have been deposited into the heart of man. These things are for those who are spiritual, who have been "born again" and are hungry for the things of God.

A lot of people have been "born again" and are going to Heaven, but they are not hungry for the things of God. It is a lot easier to get a little cake and ice cream on Sunday morning and forget about the steak. It is easier to blindly believe everything that you are told and say, "This is what our church believes," or

7

Every Believer's Authority

"This is what Dr. So-and-So says." A lot of people just go with that and never compare it with the Word of God. They never compare it! Paul said that the Spirit of God reveals these things to us. It is the Spirit of God who gets into your spirit and brings understanding, liberty, and freedom to you; but it comes through your spirit and not through your mind.

I heard a lot of preaching, and I even read the Bible before I was saved, but very little happened as a result of it because I operated solely on a mental level. Then I got hungry for God and cried out, "God, help me!" At that moment I received Jesus Christ as Lord and Savior, and admitted my human weakness. I invited God into my life for the first time, and His Holy Spirit came in and touched me. I didn't understand all the things I understand today, but the Spirit came and ministered to my spirit. My spirit came alive and I received from Him.

From that point on, whenever I read the Word, it was light to me. It was revelation to me. It began to grow in me. I got hungry and I wanted more. I wasn't satisfied with where I was. I had to find a church where they were preaching something that was out of the Word of God. When I found that church, I knew I was there. It wasn't in my head; it was in my spirit.

Sure, my head was telling me I should have stayed back where I was in the other church—it was a lot easier in the old church. There weren't any requirements on me there. There weren't any requirements to pray. There wasn't any teaching on prayer and repentance, or on living a holy life. It was a lot easier, but I wasn't saved. Every Sunday morning, a man stood up there in the pulpit and told me that if I came to church, if I was baptized in that church, I would go to Heaven. Liar! Liar! He was a liar. He will answer for it. He himself didn't know Jesus Christ as Lord, so how could he tell anyone else about Christ?

When I got into a church that preached the Word, my spirit knew I was in the right place. My flesh still wanted to go back to where it was easier, but every Sunday morning I'd get out of bed and my spirit would say, "Let's go to that church where they preach the Word." I got up thinking, "What are we going to hear today? What am I going to have to repent of today?" Oh, Lord! Everything that was dear to me I had to give up. Still, my spirit was stronger than my head. It kept drawing me to the Word. Week by week I repented, I changed, and I learned. Praise God!

You see, it is the Spirit of God who conforms us to Christ's image. The things in the Word have to come through your spirit. Jesus said we must worship God *in spirit and in truth* (see Jn. 4:24). You will hear God's Word in your ears and you will register its meaning in your brain, but you must get it down deep inside you. You have to meditate on it. You have to think about it. You have to dwell on it, ponder it, and ask the Lord, "What does that mean, Lord? How does that work, Lord?" Get real personal with Him. He

Every Believer's Authority

won't be offended. "Explain this to me, Lord. Give me understanding, Lord. Show me in Your Word, Lord." He will.

When you begin to ask the Lord to do things in you, your spirit begins to come alive and begins to override your thinking. Your spirit will begin to grow and blossom. That is what Paul is talking about.

> *But as it is written: "Eye has not seen, nor ear heard, nor have entered into the heart of man the things which God has prepared for those who love Him." But God has revealed them to us through His Spirit. For the Spirit searches all things, yes, the deep things of God. For what man knows the things of a man except the spirit of the man which is in him? Even so no one knows the things of God except the Spirit of God. Now we have received, not the spirit of the world, but the Spirit who is from God, that we might know the things that have been freely given to us by God* (1 Corinthians 2:9-12).

We receive healing and walk in divine health by repeating what the Word of God says. This is how you keep your finances in line. By repeating what the Word of God says about your finances, you begin to believe it, and then you act in accordance with it. I am not saying you should just take a Scripture out of context and stand on it. There has to be a foundation for the Scripture.

In Philippians 4:19 the apostle Paul says, "And my God shall supply all your need according to His riches in glory by Christ Jesus." Well, go back and read the first five or six verses before that. Why did Paul write this? He wrote this powerful promise to the Philippians because they were givers. He wrote it because they had been so abundantly good to him.

Paul was saying, "You have been progressing the Kingdom and helping to finance the preaching of the Word. *Because of that*, my God shall supply all your needs according to His riches in glory by Christ Jesus. There is no limit to what He will do because you have done what you are supposed to do." So, if you are going to spout Philippians 4:19, you had better make sure you are *doing* the things mentioned five verses before that. Amen! Don't just get out there on a little bitty rubber raft and float around in the water without an anchor. Get grounded on the solid Word. Also, when you stand on God's Word for healing, deliverance, finances, or any other need, apply your life to God's Word.

God's Word gives us authority over sickness. God's words are medicine and health to us. In the natural when you go to the doctor (I can't remember the last time I went to a doctor, and I don't plan on going, either, praise God!), and you have some illness in your body, he might give you a prescription.

What do you do with that prescription? Do you ignore it, or do you just read it and lay it down? Of course not! You immediately go to a pharmacist and

Every Believer's Authority

lay out $25 or $30 dollars for a couple dozen pills. Then, every day at eight o'clock you take one of those pills. Again at four o'clock that afternoon, you take one of those pills. You may do that for six or seven days until those pills are gone. What you are doing is repeating the treatment; you are repeating the dose of that medicine. That is exactly what you are to do with God's Word, for it is medicine and life.

My son, give attention to my words; incline your ear to my sayings. Do not let them depart from your eyes; keep them in the midst of your heart; for they are life to those who find them, and health to all their flesh (Proverbs 4:20-22).

A doctor's pills work on the physical body. Those pills have nothing to do with the spiritual man; they just work on the cells and organs of the body. That's fine. But think of what happens when you take God's Word as your medicine and you repeat it day in and day out. David said that he praised the Lord in the morning, at noon, and at night (see Ps. 55:17). When he laid on his bed at night, he was still praising God. He was repeating the things of God (see Ps. 63:6).

You see, God's Word is life and health. Isn't that wonderful? His Word is medicine to your body, but it works through the spirit. You will hear it in your mind, but you must get it down inside you. Take it daily!

Chapter 2

Every Believer's Authority

Spiritual authority changes lives and destinies. One time a man attended a Sunday service at our church. His life was about to change forever, and his experience would impact the lives of thousands. After my sermon, I almost always take time to pray for the people. I give a salvation and rededication call first, but quite often the gift of the word of knowledge is in operation. I will call out different sicknesses or situations that people may be experiencing as the Holy Spirit reveals things to me. (The Lord does this to show individuals who are in need that He knows about their secret need, and it builds up faith in them to believe and receive their healing.)

This particular man was a believer who attended another full-gospel church in our city. He needed a healing in a big way, and he was scheduled for surgery the following morning for arterial sclerosis. He had had a stroke shortly before this and was living on

13

Every Believer's Authority

borrowed time. At the end of the service I invited people to come forward for prayer if they needed a healing touch from God.

This man came forward, and when I layed my hands on him, the power of God knocked him to the floor. God restored his health to him instantly. When he got back on his feet his face was aglow, and all he could say was, "I feel wonderful." The surgery was cancelled, and this man told so many people about his miracle that the story was splashed across the front page of our daily newspaper! This is what appeared in *The Ashland Daily Press,* on May 25, 1991:

Prayer and Faith Brings
Ashland Man a Miracle

Dave Smith[*] is convinced the healing he has experienced is a "miracle of God." He and his wife, who are Ashland residents, believe the miracle was brought about by prayer and faith.

Dave had met Bill Ferg, pastor of the Living Faith Christian Center, Ashland, through one of the church's outreaches. About mid-January he decided to attend a service at the center. When Pastor Ferg called for those with problems to come forward for his prayer of healing, Dave responded. "I went forward to have Rev. Ferg pray for my vascular problem.

---

[*]   Names have been changed.

Every Believer's Authority

"As he was praying over me, I passed out under the power of the Holy Spirit. When I came to, I felt like the whole world was lifted off my shoulders." He continued, "When I came home, my wife knew something had happened. She must have seen the glory in my face." I told her, "I think my blood pressure and things are all taken care of."

He took his blood pressure. "It was normal for the first time in five years, and it's been stable and close to normal ever since."

Dave said, "Hope is like wishing for something. Faith is believing it's going to be. The stronger your faith, the better the results."

On February 12, he was admitted for surgery to the VA Hospital in Minneapolis, undergoing examinations and many tests during an eight-day stay. "Every day after whatever tests they gave me, the doctors would go into conference and come back and tell me they were puzzled. They asked me more questions and examined me again. Nothing in their examinations or tests showed I had a stroke. My cholesterol was high, though, and they gave me medication to control it." The doctors finally decided that surgery wouldn't be necessary, according to this man.

At this writing, this man still remains in health today. The last doctor wrote "Miracle" across the file and released him.

Every Believer's Authority

That church, Living Faith Christian Center, has gained a reputation in Northern Wisconsin and part of northern Michigan as "the church where miracles still happen." Many people drive 40 to 65 miles one way just to attend services each Sunday. *The power of God will bring people to Jesus Christ.* We don't preach a compromising or comfortable message so we can build our attendance. The message is always preached with love, though, and we rely on the conviction of the Holy Spirit and His demonstration of power to confirm the Word we preach (see Mk. 16:20).

Our Authority

Our authority in the spiritual and physical realms is an inherent right given to us when we become born again through God's Spirit. It automatically becomes "part of the package" when we believe God and become His child. However, we have to exercise it to benefit from it. We have to operate in it.

The Word shows us in First Timothy 1:18, "This charge I commit to you, son Timothy, according to the prophecies previously made concerning you, that by them you may wage the good warfare."

We are to live and think like soldiers. We are to be military-minded! I was never in the military, but I know a little bit about it. Members of the U.S. Marine Corps know who they are and what they can do. They have been given authority to bear arms, and to exert deadly military force against other nations or forces upon command. Their authority comes from the highest executive authority in the land, the President of the United States.

As Christians we too need to be military-minded. We also have authority to bear our weapons and armor to exert spiritual force "...against principalities, against powers, against the rulers of the darkness of this age, against spiritual hosts of wickedness in the heavenly places" (Eph. 6:12). Our authority comes directly from the highest authority in the universe, God the Father. If you haven't caught on yet, He means business when it comes to destroying the works of the enemy, satan.

We're in a Battle

We need to think in terms of victory. We must see things as God sees them. We should not have an attitude that says, "Oh well, it doesn't make any difference. We are going to get out of this mess anyway when Jesus comes back." No! We need to understand that we are in a battle. We are in a fight, and we need to take hold of our God-given authority and *do something* about it! Until the Lord returns, Christians shouldn't retreat—they should only advance. I understand that Jesus has won the battle, but until He comes back, we will have to enforce the devil's defeat with the Word of God.

I like living with that kind of attitude. I like to live with a little bit of fight in me! I don't know about you, but I like to use everything God has given me, including His authority. As Christians, we need to have that fight within us. We need to have that fighting, "no

Every Believer's Authority

quitting" desire to take charge over satan and cast down his evil devices and schemes. We need to keep him under our feet because it is our right. We need to keep him in check so he won't constantly run us around and control our lives. Believe me, if you don't take authority over your life and situation, the devil will! He will push you and push you until he has you beat down, discouraged, and defeated.

You can do one of two things today. First, you can allow the devil to win. Then you will live a miserable life of defeat like millions of people in the world today. Look at all the broken lives, destroyed marriages, and troubled teens around you. This is all the result of satan's pushy, hate-filled schemes and bullying in the lives of people who can't or won't do anything to stop him. The second choice—the choice Jesus provided for you on the cross at Calvary—is for you to act on the Word of God, to accept and apply the authority of Jesus Christ over your life and circumstances! You can be a conqueror and live a victorious life because that is God's plan for you.

You have to make the choice, though. I can't do it for you, and neither can your pastor or your spouse. You need to believe a strong gospel in your heart and mind. The Bible is not weak, but powerful. It has been given to you to make you the same way.

We have been given a place at the right hand of God with Jesus Christ, our Savior. We need to stand and operate in our position and power like we are sons and daughters of God with "throne room privileges."

Which He worked in Christ when He raised Him from the dead and seated Him at His right hand in the heavenly places, ... And raised us up together, and made us sit together in the heavenly places in Christ Jesus (Ephesians 1:20; 2:6).

What does the word *authority* really mean? *The American Heritage Dictionary* (American Heritage Publishing Company, Inc. and Houghton Mifflin Company of New York, 1971) says authority means "(1) the right and power to command, enforce laws, exact obedience, determine, or judge; (2) a person or group invested with this right and power; (3) power delegated to others; authorization."

We have authority, but what are we supposed to do with it? Jesus said, "...'All authority has been given to Me in heaven and on earth. Go therefore...' " (Mt. 28:18-19). Whenever you see the word *therefore*, you should automatically go to the previous verse to see what it was "there for." In verse 18, Jesus said all authority was given to Him in Heaven and earth. By linking the "cause" in verse 18 with the "effect" in verse 19, we can see that Jesus was saying, "Because I have all authority, then I want you to go in My name and make disciples who will follow Me."

What do we do with these disciples once they believe and receive? Look to the Scriptures: "Teaching them to observe all things that I have commanded you; and lo, I am with you always, even to the end of the age..." (Mt. 28:20). These things require authority. Supernatural faith cannot be passed down

Every Believer's Authority

through dusty textbooks or empty vessels who deny the power of their Lord. True spiritual authority births authority in others.

What "things" should we tell these new disciples about? First, we should tell them about Jesus Christ, the author and finisher of their faith. Acts 10:38 says, "...God anointed Jesus of Nazareth with the Holy Spirit and with power, who went about doing good and healing all who were oppressed by the devil, for God was with Him."

Something even more shocking happened in the life of Jesus: the dead obeyed Him and came back to life! As believers and disciples of Jesus Christ, we have the same authority that He demonstrated on the earth! Some might say, "Oh, Bill, now you have gone too far." No! I haven't gone far enough, and I hope you'll get a hold of this and really find out what God's Word says. Look at what Jesus said in the Gospel of John:

> *Most assuredly, I say to you, he who believes in Me, the works that I do he will do also; and greater works then these he will do, because I go to My Father. And whatever you ask in My name, that I will do, that the Father may be glorified in the Son. If you ask anything in My name, I will do it* (John 14:12-14).

In the Gospel of Matthew, Jesus said something just as shocking: "And as you go, preach, saying, 'The kingdom of heaven is at hand.' Heal the sick, cleanse the lepers, raise the dead, cast out demons. Freely you have received, freely give" (Mt. 10:7-8). Is it rare to see the dead raised in our day? Absolutely. (It was even rare in Jesus' day.) Is it impossible? Absolutely not!

Jesus said we would do the same things He did—and even greater things! This isn't so we can brag about how spiritual we are. No! The purpose for the power is for the Father to be glorified in the Son. Every time you operate in the authority that Jesus Christ gave you through His death and resurrection, your heavenly Father is glorified. When demons are cast out and the sick are healed, your heavenly Father receives glory.

During a crusade I held in Uganda in East Africa, I was traveling by car through the city of Kampala when we came upon an accident. An elderly lady had been struck by a hit and run driver and left for dead in the street.

When I saw her lying there I told my driver to stop the car because I wanted to pray for her. The driver said, "It's too late; she's dead." "Yes, I know," I said, "That's why I want to pray."

The anointing was so powerful at that time that I knew the lady was going to live. When the anointing comes on me I know that God is going to do something great—someone will be healed or delivered.

The driver stopped the car and by the time we got to the accident scene the lady's body had been pulled off to the side of the street. She was bleeding from her nose, mouth, and ears, and the back of her head was cracked open and bleeding.

Immediately I layed hands on her and began to command her life to return in the name of Jesus. I rebuked the spirit of death. Within moments she was breathing and moving about. We all continued to pray, and in five minutes she was sitting up. After that the ambulance took her away to the hospital. I give God all the glory. I'm so thankful for His Word that tells me my authority is in Jesus name. Matthew 10:8 tells us to heal the sick, cleanse the lepers, raise the dead, and cast out demons. Freely we have received; freely we should give.

Believers Cast Out Demons

Jesus Christ believes in "hands-on" training and instruction. He didn't just talk to His followers about spiritual authority; He sent them out to "do it" in person! The Gospel of Luke records the story and the important truth Jesus drove home to the 70 disciples when they came back from their "home mission trip" rejoicing over the fact that the demons were subject to them.

Then the seventy returned with joy, saying, "Lord, even the demons are subject to us in Your name." And He said to them, "I saw Satan fall like lightning from heaven. Behold, I give you the authority to trample on serpents and scorpions, and over all the power of the enemy, and nothing shall by any means hurt you" (Luke 10:17-19).

Jesus called satan and his demons "serpents and scorpions" and the "enemy." In the next verse, His words and tone deliver two key messages to His disciples then and now: "Nevertheless do not rejoice in this, that the spirits are subject to you, but rather rejoice because your names are written in heaven" (Lk. 10:20). First, Jesus redirected the disciples' focus from their power to their Source and identity. Second, His matter-of-fact tone told the disciples that this kind of authority and miraculous operation shouldn't be considered unusual—it should be commonplace. Every believer should do it.

The Church is weak and sickly today because it hasn't exercised the authority Jesus gave it. It hasn't exercised its authority. It hasn't used its authority. It hasn't walked in its authority. Thus it created a "power vacuum" that allowed satan to bring in his own set of devilish doctrines to keep the church from discovering and recovering the truth of God's Word. How does satan get into the Church? It's simple. He enters the door through believers who don't know their authority. He infiltrates the Church through unbelievers who call themselves believers, and through anybody who will listen to him.

He emasculates the Church by weakening individuals through attacks of the mind. Satan gets into our churches through people by attacking their minds through the temptations, specific thoughts, and illicit pleasures he sows in our minds. Is it God's job to clean the room of your mind every day? No! It is our

Every Believer's Authority

job to cast down every ungodly thought, and to take the things we hear or think and check them with the Word.

For the weapons of our warfare are not carnal but mighty in God for pulling down strongholds, casting down arguments and every high thing that exalts itself against the knowledge of God, bringing every thought into captivity to the obedience of Christ (2 Corinthians 10:4-5).

The Bible Is Our Guide

I hope you take down notes and write down Scriptures. Check out what I say here, and verify it in your Bible. If you are not sure about something, ask the Lord to show you. Don't just take everything I say as gospel. Prove it. Prove it to yourself through the Word of God.

There is a direct correlation between a lawyer and a preacher in the sense that a lawyer has to defend his client, while a preacher defends the gospel. It is my job to build up and defend the Word of God. What kind of lawyer would go into a courtroom with his client and say, "Your honor and members of the jury, I don't know what I think of this guy. My client might be innocent, or he might be guilty. Now do what you want with him." That is the way a lot of preaching is today: "This is how many people view the Bible. Now, it may be truth and may not. Do what you want with it." Oh, how wrong can people be! The Word of

24

God is alive, true, and powerful—and it will change the life of a person who was damned to hell.

As a minister of the gospel, I have to defend the Word. I have to declare: "It doesn't say anything less than this. This is the Word of God, and this is how we have to look at the Word. No, it is not just a pretty story. It is not just an interesting thing that was written. It is Truth. It is power, and it is light. That is the way we must approach it. You must understand that what God has said in His Word; He will back it up!"

All Scripture is given by inspiration of God, and is profitable for doctrine, for reproof, for correction, for instruction in righteousness, that the man of God may be complete, thoroughly equipped for every good work (2 Timothy 3:16-17).

False Doctrines of the Last Days

The apostle Paul prophesied about the last days in First Timothy 4:1 "Now the Spirit expressly says that in latter times some will depart from the faith, giving heed to deceiving spirits and doctrines of demons" (2 Tim. 3:1-2,5-6). In his second letter to Timothy, Paul warned:

But know this, that in the last days perilous times will come: for men will be lovers of themselves, lovers of money, boasters, proud, blasphemers, disobedient to parents, unthankful, unholy, ... having a form of godliness but denying its power. And from such

*people turn away! For of this sort are those
who creep into households and make captives
of gullible women loaded down with sins, led
away by various lusts* (2 Timothy 3:1-2,5-6).

In verse 5 Paul says that in the last days, there will
be a "form of godliness" or a form of religion that de-
nies the power of God; he predicts that many false
doctrines will come along. The devil is doing everything he can to deceive you, to get you to think
wrong things. He will stoop to almost anything to rob
you of your zeal and your fire for God. He wants you
to lose your courage and ability to fight. He knows he
has won if he can get you to stop praying, or at least
to stop praying against him.

You and I are the greatest problem that satan has
on the earth. To accomplish his evil works, he must
contend with the saints of God who are endued with
power and authority to rein on the earth! He knows
that where there is no Word of God, he has free reign.
The atmosphere in certain Third World countries, in
places where the Word of God is not preached, is absolutely demonic. You can literally feel the demons in
these countries, and you sense their presence everywhere. We don't have that so much in America because the Word is being preached and because a
significant number of strong Christians are here. I
must say also that there are many places in America
under the power of satan. You will find most of these
places in our large cities. This is where Christians

Every Believer's Authority

need to go. We need to get out of the pews and get praying and preaching in these devilish places!

In those Third World nations where preachers and missionaries answered God's call and preached the uncompromised Word of God, the powers of satan diminished over time and miracles happened in abundance. Thousands of people have been saved and set free from satan's clutches. The Lord has given us power and authority to witness and live the Christian life. It takes boldness to live an uncompromising Christian life. It also takes the authority of God.

Doctrine of Demons

Another example of the doctrine of demons in operation is in the area of church attendance. People spend a lot of time and energy coming up wtih new excuses for not going to church. They don't know it, but they're getting some supernatural help with their excuse-making. "I will go when I feel like it. If I get there once a month, that is enough." Now, who do you suppose is *really* doing the talking here?

Do you think Jesus Christ would say you don't have to go to church? "No, you don't have to come and hear about Me, and you definitcly don't have to come and worship Me. Don't worry about getting together with your brothers and sisters—you don't have to be a part of My family gathering. You can just stay in your bed at home and watch TV. Maybe you can work on your house of worship—I mean, 'sail' your boat." The attitude that says, "Well, I don't have to go," is a doctrine of demons. The devil wants you out

Every Believer's Authority

of church so you are separated from the flock and easy prey for his many devices of evil. The Lord of lords has a different opinion.

You may say, "I can't find a church that is spiritual enough." Well, get in there with your brethren and pray anyway! Maybe it will get spiritual enough for you. "You know, the people just aren't friendly to me." In your wisdom and in your private study of God's Word, did you ever run across Proverbs 18:24? "A man who has friends must himself be friendly" (Prov. 18:24a). Go and be friendly to the people at church, and maybe, just maybe, they will get friendly with you. They have to see somebody who is friendly first of all, so give them an example of friendliness. No matter how many excuses people concoct to justify why they don't want to go to church, they are still trapped in an outright doctrine of demons that directly contradicts the Word of God in Hebrews 10:24-25:

And let us consider one another in order to stir up love and good works, not forsaking the assembling of ourselves together, as is the manner of some, but exhorting one another, and so much the more as you see the Day approaching.

The Bible states God's case in black and white for all to see: We should be in church and in Bible studies even more as the day of the Lord approaches! Acts 20:28 says Jesus purchased the Church with His own blood. That's a high price to pay. We can't take it lightly.

Hear the Truth

What are the facts about our authority over satan? Do we have authority in the heavenlies? Do we have the authority to bind up the strong man? Do we have the authority to bind up religious demons in our geographical areas?

Put on the whole armor of God, that you may be able to stand against the wiles of the devil [that is trickery, cunningness, and craftiness]. *For we do not wrestle against flesh and blood, but against principalities, against powers, against the rulers of the darkness of this age, against spiritual hosts of wickedness in the heavenly places* (Ephesians 6:11-12).

Paul revealed more information about these "heavenly places" in his second letter to the Corinthians. Paul said he knew a man (speaking of himself), who was caught up into "the third heaven" and entered into the throne room of God (see 2 Cor. 12:2). There are different levels in the heavenlies; our atmosphere is the "first heaven." I believe there is a second heaven occupied by the spiritual hosts of wickedness and satan himself. It is beyond us. It is also beyond our spaceships, I imagine. There is also the third heaven described by Paul, which is the home of God's throne in the spiritual realm.

We will not see these things with the naked eye, but we need to understand that satan has set up a military operation complete with officers and infantry, with different levels of authority and demonic operation, on the earth and in the heavenlies. I believe that

Every Believer's Authority

the throne of satan, and his ruling demons, resides in the heavenly realm right now. Their orders then go forth to demons operating in our realm.

Believers Have Authority Over All Devils

When the 70 disciples excitedly reported to Jesus that even the demons were subject to them in His name, He just said He had watched satan fall like a bolt of lightning from Heaven (see Lk. 10:18b). He didn't even have to participate in the "fight"—it was over before it started. Satan was, and is, just a *created being*, an angel of light who willfully turned to utter darkness. Scripture says, "For this purpose the Son of God was manifested, that He might destroy the works of the devil" (1 Jn. 3:8b). Our Lord has complete and total mastery over the adversary. It is *not an even match*—we have no reason to be intimidated or dismayed. When the Word is preached and people are in prayer, the power of satan is broken. We have to believe that. We have to take that authority over the devil and his evil devices. Our authority over satan and his demons is manifested when we pray. Share the Word of God with the unsaved.

Maybe you just don't see it because you don't see manifestations of your God-given authority immediately, but that doesn't mean it isn't happening. Satan knows if you believe or don't. He knows if you are just mouthing things, or if you have the conviction you need in your heart to take genuine authority over him. Take that authority and trust in God. When you trust what God has said, He will back you up.

Believe You Receive

The Lord gave me this word one morning as I was praying: "Be faithful to Me, My children, as I am faithful to you. Do I not hear you when you cry out to Me? Listen to Me when I speak to you." We have the assurance that God hears what we pray and what we say. He wants to give us the desires of our hearts. I guarantee that when we are in a spiritual battle, we have all the hosts in Heaven and the power of our heavenly Father Himself behind us. It is not a matter of praying, "Oh God, will You please back me up if I cast out this devil?" His faithfulness is beyond question. His tesimony is only "yes and amen" (see 2 Cor. 1:20).

When you operate according to spiritual principles and laws, when you operate in God's Word, you can be sure that God will "back you up." Don't give in. Don't cave in. Don't look at the circumstances, but look at the Word of God. Know that the Truth hasn't changed because of your situation. We are in a war. God's saints are warring against the devil's demons, and the spoils of war are the souls of men. Don't let the word *war* scare you; I assure you that "they" have much more to fear than we do. Of course, they will try to plant fear in you, but don't take it. (See Second Timothy 1:7.)

The Lord Has Given Us Power!

If you love Me, keep My commandments. And I will pray the Father, and He will give you another Helper, that He may abide with you

Every Believer's Authority

forever—the Spirit of truth, whom the world cannot receive, because it neither sees Him nor knows Him; but you know Him, for He dwells with you and will be in you (John 14:15-17).

Jesus promised to send us "another Helper," who is the Holy Spirit, to dwell with us. He said the world would not know or receive Him, but we would. Jesus told the disciples even more about the Holy Spirit just before He ascended to Heaven in the Book of Acts:

"For John truly baptized with water, but you shall be baptized with the Holy Spirit not many days from now." Therefore, when they had come together, they asked Him, saying, "Lord, will You at this time restore the king-dom to Israel?" And He said to them, "It is not for you to know times or seasons which the Father has put in His own authority. But you shall receive power when the Holy Spirit has come upon you; and you shall be witnesses to Me in Jerusalem, and in all Judea and Sama-ria, and to the end of the earth" (Acts 1:5-8).

In the Book of Acts, Jesus adds some astounding new information to the things He said about the Holy Spirit in John 14:15-17. He says that *power* will come to those who believe when the Holy Spirit comes upon them. This *power* (translated from the Greek word, *dunamis*, from which we get the English word *dyna-mite*) is given so we can boldly witness about Jesus with authority. Acts 2:1-4 records the fulfillment of

His promise on the Day of Pentecost with the baptism of the Holy Spirit in the upper room with 120 people speaking in other tongues (the initial evidence of the baptism in the Holy Spirit in the biblical record).

Peter proclaimed the news of this new outpouring to his fellow Jews in in Acts 2:38-40:

Then Peter said to them, "Repent, and let every one of you be baptized in the name of Jesus Christ for the remission of sins; and you shall receive the gift of the Holy Spirit. For the promise is to you and to your children, and to all who are afar off, as many as the Lord our God will call." And with many other words he testified and exhorted them, saying, "Be saved from this perverse generation."

Contrary to popular fundamental teaching, this experience didn't end after the disciples and apostles had all died. Peter said by the Holy Spirit in verse 39, "For the promise is to you and to your children, and to all who are afar off...." Peter wasn't referring to people who were far off in distance, but far off in years.

Two thousand years later, the supernatural baptism of the Holy Spirit is still happening. In fact, more than 400 million Christians worldwide have been baptized in the Holy Spirit with the evidence of speaking in tongues! If you dare to ask the Lord for the baptism in the Holy Spirit, He will fill you. Carefully read the Book of Acts, and keep in mind the fact that according to God's Word, these things are for today.

The Word Is Your Weapon

God has given us His Word as our greatest offensive weapon against satan, but we have to use it. We must preach it and exercise it. Anytime you hear preaching that diminishes the Word of God and the power of the gospel, you are hearing a doctrine of demons. Things that lessen the Word are simply doctrines of demons. Anytime you hear someone say something contrary to the revealed Word and will of God, something like, "Well, you don't want to be believing too much for healing," or "Well, you shouldn't be messing around casting out devils. You don't pray against the devil because he will come and get you!"

I'm sorry, but my Bible still says, "You are of God, little children, and have overcome them [evil spirits, false prophets, and the spirit of antichrist], because He who is in you is greater than he who is in the world" (1 Jn. 4:4)! You have to know God's Word so you can accurately discern when something is wrong with a man's teaching or statements. I was brought up in a church where we never talked about the devil. When we did talk about him, we just whispered. We figured that if we said it too loud, he would come to "get us." I got tired of living like that. I have authority over the devil. I am going to show you in God's Word that you have authority *over the devil*. He is subject to you.

Another false doctrine that we often hear is, "You don't have to read the Bible; God will talk to you. He will lead you and show you what to do." That is a lie.

Every Believer's Authority

You do need to read your Bible. God worked through the sacrificed lives and shed blood of prophets and apostles to bring His written Word to us. Jesus Christ, the Son of God, based all His ministry on the *written* Word of God in the Old Testament. The apostle Paul wrote this to Timothy, the young pastor he personally trained up for the ministry:

All Scripture is given by inspiration of God, and is profitable for doctrine, for reproof, for correction, for instruction in righteousness, that the man of God may be complete, thoroughly equipped for every good work (2 Timothy 3:16-17).

Any man or woman who shuns the Bible and tries to operate on personal revelation alone will be incomplete and poorly equipped to do good works before God. You must receive the ingrafted Word of God: "…and receive with meekness the implanted word, which is able to save your souls" (Jas. 1:21). In the Gospel of John, Jesus said the Holy Spirit would "teach you all things, and bring to your remembrance all things that I said to you" (Jn. 14:26). If there are no holy words implanted in you, He can't bring anything to your remembrance!

You must have the Word of God implanted within you first, and then you are responsible to be a "doer of the word" and not a hearer only (see Jas. 1:23). To continually be refreshed and renewed, you must get yourself full of the Word. You cannot go along saying,

35

Every Believer's Authority

"I just read a couple of chapters just last month!" and expect them to carry you through to the next month. You need to read a couple of chapters every day. You need to get built up every day in the Word of God!

Chapter 3

Our Authority
Comes From Heaven

On a mission trip to Guyana, South America, I traveled to different churches sharing the gospel. In each service, I witnessed the power of the Holy Spirit manifested in the same way we read about in the Book of Acts and in others places throughout the Bible. In the Gospel of Mark, we are shown what we should expect to see when we believe and tell others about the Lord.

And they went out and preached everywhere, the Lord working with them and confirming the word through the accompanying signs. Amen (Mark 16:20).

In each church where I preached, people were saved, healed, and filled with the Holy Spirit. However, in one particular Friday night service, I was coming to the end of a long healing line when a small

Every Believer's Authority

lady who was about 27 years old, came up for prayer. She told me she "felt confusion" in her head, and I could tell by her actions that she was distressed and irritated by it, and that she had no control over her condition.

When I laid my hands on her and prayed, she began to repent and ask God to forgive her. I sensed that she needed more prayer and possibly deliverance, so I sent her back to her seat along with one of the other ministers who had come with me. I continued praying for the other people in the line, but after a short while, this lady started getting very loud. I walked back to where she was sitting and spoke to her, and immediately she opened her mouth and began to bray like a donkey!

We led this young woman to the front of the church and instructed the people to intercede as we cast the demon out of her. The lady's name was Marjorie,[*] but when I called her by name, the voice of a demon spoke to me. I asked the demon what its name was, and where it came from. The thing replied, "I am Veren, and I come from the ocean." Then a terrible string of curses and filth directed at us flowed through Marjorie's mouth from the demon!

I rebuked the demon in Jesus' name, and told it that it would not speak to us like that. Demons are liars, and you don't know when they are telling the truth, so I didn't address the demon as "Veren." I only

---

[*] Name has been changed.

called it what it was—a demon or foul spirit. At times this demon would say, "I am a wicked demon," in a slow syrupy voice.

Marjorie's deliverance did not happen as quickly as some I had been involved in, but I knew of testimonies where deliverances sometimes took hours or whole days. I was determined to stick with it as long as it took. After all, I wasn't leaving for the States for four more days. At one point the Guyanese pastor wanted to stop, but I told him we couldn't and wouldn't. I had four days, but I knew it wouldn't take that long, for the Greater One was inside me.

Marjorie had been a Christian, but she had backslidden and married a Hindu man. Hinduism is one of the main religions of Guyana. The British brought in thousands of people from India over a hundred years ago to work as slaves in the sugar cane fields of Guyana. These unwilling immigrants also brought their Hindu religion with them, and it is a plague in that country today.

Satan does some of his most wicked work in the lives of backslidden Christians. When Christians turn their back on God, they give satan full authority to possess and abuse them. In many cases, they in turn abuse others in their pain. Jeffrey Dahlmer, the notorious killer who murdered young men and ate their body parts, even carried one of his victim's heads to work with him. That is the mind of satan manifesting its evil desires in the flesh. Dahlmer was a born-again Christian as a teenager and young adult. When he backslid and fell into the twisted grip of homosexuality and perversion, satan used him to inflict torture and death on other lives. (Review Luke 11:24-26.)

The pastor of this church in Guyana said "Veren" was the name of a local Hindu god. Women who wanted to become pregnant would go to the ocean or river and bring offerings of food and gifts to this Hindu god, then they would become pregnant. Marjorie was pregnant, but she was also demon-possessed.

The demon in this woman kept asking for water (demons always want water), but I refused it water and commanded it to come out in Jesus' name. I told it to return where it came from. Every so often Marjorie would bray like a donkey and her face would contort and change in appearance. The demon often tried to speak out with incredible hate and contempt, but each time we rebuked it in Jesus' name. It would always obey us. At one point the demon said he would leave at 12:10 if I left him alone; sometimes they try to make a deal. I replied, "No! You're coming out now."

For several days before that meeting, the Lord had been giving me the Scripture passage in Philippians 2:8-10, yet I wasn't able to preach it. I wondered why I kept hearing it:

And being found in appearance as a man, He humbled Himself and became obedient to the point of death, even the death of the cross. Therefore God also has highly exalted Him and given Him the name which is above every name, that at the name of Jesus every knee should bow, of those in heaven, and of those on earth, and of those under the earth (Philippians 2:8-10).

During this deliverance, this passage kept coming back to me. Then I understood the reason. Verse 10 says, "That at the name of Jesus every knee should bow, of those in heaven, and of those on earth, and of those under the earth." Those under the earth shall bow to Jesus. Then I said to the demon, "God's Word says that you will bow your knee to the name of Jesus Christ, and I command you now to do so." For the first time, the demon was silent. Then one of the pastors pushed on Marjorie's shoulder, as if to apply a little pressure so she would bow. But the demon snapped at the pastor and said, "Don't force me. You can't force me."

Then I knew that I was on to something. This proud, haughty demon had shown fear. It knew what God's Word said! I gently walked Marjorie over to the church platform, where two steps led up to the pulpit. When her toes bumped into the bottom step, she wasn't able to move forward anymore. I placed my hand on her back and gently pushed forward, and she slowly fell forward onto the platform. Her knees bent, and she was actually kneeling on the first step as she lay there.

As Marjorie lay face down, I spoke to the demon that was afflicting her. "Demon, you have just bowed

Every Believer's Authority

down to Jesus. You bowed your knees to the King of kings and the Lord of lords. Confess Jesus as Lord, demon." Some time passed and Marjorie raised herself up just enough for me to see tears flowing down her cheeks. I said, "Repeat after me, 'Jesus is Lord.' " Then I heard a whispering voice, and I asked, "Who is saying this?" The reply came back in a low whisper, "Veren." I knew the battle was over, and I immediately issued a command with the authority given to me through the Spirit of God and the blood of the Lamb: "In the name of Jesus Christ of Nazareth... come out of her!"

Marjorie began to spit up a thick, white, foamy substance. Then she looked up at a banner with big red letters over the platform that said, "Jesus is Lord," and she began to speak on her own. "Jesus is Lord. Jesus is Lord. Jesus is Lord." Again, I asked who was in there, but this time the reply was, "Marjorie." Hallelujah! She stood up and said, "Pastor, thank you," and hugged me. Then she ran over to her former pastor, called him "Pastor," and hugged him.

After her deliverance, we had her plead the blood of Jesus, and we prayed for her unborn baby. Then we had her read the first two chapters of the Gospel of John along with some other Scriptures. This immediately began the process of renewing her mind. Although the people from church had gone home, Marjorie's family was waiting for her. We carefully instructed them on how to keep her in the Word, and in church, and we showed them how to take authority over anything that would try to come back into her.

Do you know what? It wasn't 12:10 a.m.—it was only 10:30 p.m. Marjorie's deliverance didn't take four days, but if it had, I would have kept at it. Why? It is worth it to see even one captive rescued from hell! That is what Jesus did, and that is what He told His followers to do. He gave us the same power and authority He had. We can use His name over the devil, and all satan's demons are subject to us. They must obey. They will confess Jesus as Lord, and they must obey. If we start walking in the authority that became ours when we became followers of Jesus Christ, then any demons we encounter will confess that Jesus is Lord and bow their knee to Him—*starting today*, here and now!

We have been given this kind of supernatural authority and power because there is a real hell and a real devil, and he is out to steal, kill, and destroy (see Jn. 10:10). We have been given the commission to follow in the footsteps of Jesus, the same Jesus Christ who came to destroy the works of the enemy! (See First John 3:8.)

There is a real Heaven and a real God, and He is "not willing that any should perish but that all should come to repentance" (2 Pet. 3:9b). The Lord uses us to rescue mankind, and we do it by sharing the gospel, praying for the sick, and casting out demons! There is no doubt about it: Miracles are for today!

Our Authority Comes From Heaven

But God, who is rich in mercy, because of His great love with which He loved us, even when

Every Believer's Authority

we were dead in trespasses, made us alive together with Christ (by grace you have been saved), and raised us up together, and made us sit together in the heavenly places in Christ Jesus (Ephesians 2:4-6).

So we are *already* in heavenly places in Christ Jesus. We will be in Heaven both physically and supernaturally one day, but we are already there now in the spirit. We are already ruling and reigning, and our authority comes from Heaven. God says here in His Word that He sees us seated with Him. Just as the ruling demons in the second heaven give orders and give out authority, so our authority is handed down from a power and throne high above them. Our power and authority come from a Source who is over, higher, and above all; all the authority of Heaven is with us and given to us.

Even though we live on a physical plane in the first heaven and demonic forces rule and reign in the second heaven above us, they are still subject to us in the name of Jesus Christ! They have to listen to us. Doesn't the Word in Ephesians 2:6 say that you and I are seated in heavenly places in Christ Jesus? When Jesus spoke to demons, they were subject to Him. They answered His questions, and they didn't "talk back." They didn't turn around and walk away either. They tried to hide, but they always lost. They always obeyed. So it is with us. When Jesus left He put us in charge. He said, "All authority has been given to Me in heaven and on earth" (Mt. 28:18b). Now Jesus Christ

44

is in Heaven interceding for us, and the authority He wielded in the earth has been given to us. We have authority in Heaven and on earth. When we pray, the Father hears and answers us. He honors the authority He has delegated to us when we speak to those demon powers. They must listen to us because that authority has been given to us by the Most High God, and they know who we represent. Whenever you intercede for your city, your nation, or another person, your prayers enter into heavenly places.

I remember hearing testimonies of American Christians who visited the former Soviet Union in the late 1970's and during the 1980's. Different ones told me that they would always go to the Kremlin in Red Square in Moscow. It's a massive, ominous structure; I've seen it myself. These Christians would always walk around the Kremlin and bind up the spirits of Communism and command them to come down and loose that nation. It didn't happen overnight, but over the years you could see those demons losing their hold on the nation. By 1990, Communism had toppled. It was not because of economics, as the world thought; it was a spiritual battle and God's people won.

In many cities where a Christian crusade was to be held, prayer warriors would go in one or two weeks before to bind up territorial demons. The results of those crusades have always been great—with revival fires buring high. This is our authority. Yet there must also be the leading of the Holy Spirit in this type of

Every Believer's Authority

praying. We must remain scriptural and not get "flaky."

I'm reminded of Luke 10 when Jesus sent 70 others out to preach with authority. Verse 17 says, "Then the seventy returned with joy, saying, 'Lord, even the demons are subject to us in Your name.' " Then in verse 18 Jesus replied, "I saw Satan fall like lightning from heaven." This could mean two things. First, Jesus saw satan fall from Heaven (God's Kingdom) many years before when satan was thrown out in rebellion against God. By saying this, Jesus was telling these 70 preachers that they had triumphed over satan because he was powerless when they used Jesus' name against him. The second thing Jesus' reply in verse 18 could mean is that as the disciples preached the Kingdom of God and prayed, their authority overpowered satan and cast him out of his throne in the heavenlies.

I think Jesus was saying both of these things. The bottom line is, we have been given all authority over satan and his demons, according to Luke 10:19. So don't try to explain the authority away. Operate in the authority Jesus gave you. Jesus said in Matthew 16:19, "And I will give you the keys of the kingdom of heaven, and whatever you bind on earth will be bound in heaven, and whatever you loose on earth will be loosed in heaven."

How you are fallen from heaven, O Lucifer, son of the morning! How you are cut down to the ground, you who weakened the nations!

For you have said in your heart: "I will ascend into heaven, I will exalt my throne above the stars of God; I will also sit in the mount of the congregation on the farthest sides of the north; I will ascend above the heights of the clouds, I will be like the Most High." Yet you shall be brought down to Sheol, to the lowest depths of the Pit. Those who see you will gaze at you, and consider you, saying: "Is this the man who made the earth tremble, who shook kingdoms, who made the world as a wilderness and destroyed its cities, who did not open the house of his prisoners?" (Isaiah 14:12-17)

The Bible says people will be amazed at what the devil really is when they see him on Judgment Day. Many of us will wish we had been bolder for God. It's never too late to exercise your position in Christ, though!

Have the Nature of God

If God's authority is going to work in our lives, then we must find out what God says and expects in the area of holiness. We are to be Christlike, having the divine nature of God in us.

Or do you not know that your body is the temple of the Holy Spirit who is in you, whom you have from God, and you are not your own? (1 Corinthians 6:19)

You are of God, little children, and have overcome them, because He who is in you is

Every Believer's Authority

greater than he who is in the world (1 John 4:4).

Peter bluntly tells us to follow the steps and example of Jesus:

For to this you were called, because Christ also suffered for us, leaving us an example, that you should follow His steps: "Who committed no sin, nor was deceit found in His mouth"; who, when He was reviled, did not revile in return; when He suffered, He did not threaten, but committed Himself to Him who judges righteously; who Himself bore our sins in His own body on the tree, that we, having died to sins, might live for righteousness—by whose stripes you were healed. For you were like sheep going astray, but have now returned to the Shepherd and Overseer of your souls (1 Peter 2:21-25).

Grace and peace be multiplied to you in the knowledge of God and of Jesus our Lord, as His divine power has given to us all things that pertain to life and godliness, through the knowledge of Him who called us by glory and virtue, by which have been given to us exceedingly great and precious promises, that through these you may be partakers of the divine nature, having escaped the corruption that is in the world through lust. But also for this very reason, giving all diligence, add to your faith virtue, to virtue knowledge, to knowledge self-control, to self-control perseverance, to perseverance godliness, to godliness brotherly kindness, and to brotherly kindness love. For if these things are yours and abound, you will be neither barren nor unfruitful in the knowledge of our Lord Jesus Christ. For he who lacks these things is shortsighted, even to blindness, and has forgotten that he was cleansed from his old sins. Therefore, brethren, be even more diligent to make your calling and election sure, for if you do these things you will never stumble; for so an entrance will be supplied to you abundantly into the everlasting kingdom of our Lord and Savior Jesus Christ (2 Peter 1:2-11).

Verse 4 of Second Peter 1 says we can partake of His divine nature. It is not impossible to be like Jesus Christ in our behavior, thoughts, and actions. Oswald Chambers once wrote that it is what we are in the dark that counts. All the rest is reputation. God sees us in the dark: what we imagine and think. So obedience to God's Word is holiness.

In the second and third chapters of the Book of Revelation, we read about seven churches that existed during the apostle John's time. To every one of these churches, Jesus said, "I know your works." Then He goes on to reveal that most of these first century churches had sin to deal with. Jesus knows all about your life; nothing can be hidden from Him.

Repent and Be an Ambassador for Christ

The first 11 verses of Colossians 3 talk about avoiding and turning away from things as Christ's ambassadors on the earth. The next five verses (Col. 3:12-17), tell us what to "put on" and how we should act as Christians. God doesn't "leave us alone" just because we receive Jesus Christ as Savior. He persistently works in us to conform us to the image of His beloved Son (see Rom. 8:29). If the Holy Spirit is dealing with you about some hidden sin in your life, now is the best time to repent of it. Ask Jesus for forgiveness and sin no more. Ask the Holy Spirit to fill you and help you live the divine life in the way Jesus planned it for you. He hasn't planned defeat and sickness for us; He has called us to be His ambassadors, His personal representatives.

Now then we are ambassadors for Christ, as though God were pleading through us: we implore you on Christ's behalf, be reconciled to God (2 Corinthians 5:20).

As you therefore have received Christ Jesus the Lord, so walk in Him, rooted and built up in Him and established in the faith, as you have been taught, abounding in it with thanksgiving. Beware lest anyone cheat you through philosophy and empty deceit, according to the tradition of men, according to the basic principles of the world, and not according to Christ. For in Him dwells all the fullness of the

Godhead bodily; and you are complete in Him, who is the head of all principality and power (Colossians 2:6-10).

We are to "walk in Christ." We must walk in His authority, and act just like Him. Since God's Word declares that you are complete in Christ, you don't need anything more. You can accomplish whatever He has called you to do because He has transferred and delegated His power and authority to you—you are His ambassador.

In the Book of Ephesians, the apostle Paul revealed how God the Father exalted His obedient Son: "And He put all things under His feet, and gave Him to be head over all things to the church, which is His body, the fullness of Him who fills all in all" (Eph. 1:22-23). Jesus' fullness, His authority, has filled all in all. It has filled the Church, and it has filled you and I. His authority has come down into the Church of His saints. Through His authority, we have the fullness of Christ flowing and operating through us.

If this is true, then we have a long way to go! If this is true, and I believe it is, we have a long way to go to be like Christ. Does anybody understand what it is to be like Christ? Does anybody understand what it is like to operate in that love, to operate with His gifts and Spirit, and to really operate in His total authority? Do we really understand it? You and I have a long way to go, but His Word will guide us. The Holy Spirit will show us. The Lord will not let us get flaky and wander

Every Believer's Authority

off into wrong areas—if you are in His Word and His will.

In chapter 2 of the Book of Colossians, Paul teaches us more about our authority in Christ: "And you, being dead in your trespasses and the uncircumcision of your flesh, He has made alive together with Him, having forgiven you all trespasses" (Col. 2:13). Jesus Christ has made us alive with Him—not just "alive" and separate, but alive "together with Him."

The Book of Romans declares, "Therefore we were buried with Him through baptism into death, that just as Christ was raised from the dead by the glory of the Father, even so we also should walk in newness of life" (Rom. 6:4). We have been raised up with Him and given newness of life. Jesus was raised up to walk in a realm that He hadn't walked in before, and all authority was given onto Him as the Sacrificed Lamb who had risen from the dead. Now we are to walk into that realm also.

Don't Get Into the Flesh

Another danger area lies in wait on the edge of this truth about the authority of believers in the earth. Several years ago, some teaching surfaced and triggered some excessive behavior that got into the flesh. People actually began to teach and believe they could "fight the devil" in the flesh. With their language and body movements they acted like they were physically "wrestling with the devil." "Devil, I got you now. I am going to kill you." There was one big problem with that: it was not scriptural. Most of these people don't do this anymore because respected leaders in the Body of Christ went to them and said, "Look, brethren, this is an error." In the end, they received godly counsel, repented of their error, and got straightened out.

For though we walk in the flesh, we do not war according to the flesh. For the weapons of our warfare are not carnal but mighty in God for pulling down strongholds (2 Corinthians 10:3-4).

The apostle Paul made it very clear that we are not fighting against flesh and blood, and that the weapons of our warfare are not carnal or fleshly, but are mighty and powerful. He lists our weapons and armor in great detail in Ephesians 6:11-18, and nowhere on the list do our fists show up.

Yet Michael the archangel, in contending with the devil, when he disputed about the body of Moses, dared not bring against him a reviling accusation, but said, "The Lord rebuke you!" (Jude 9)

Jude is saying here that Michael did not bring railings or abusive words against satan. We do not have to rail at the devil; we don't have to make all kinds of wild accusations. You can call him an old snake if you want to: "Satan, you snake. You filthy spirit." You can address him, but don't go fighting against him. Don't make accusations or railings because you will not upset him in the least. He will not get hurt, and it will

Every Believer's Authority

not do any good. In fact, I suppose he kind of likes to be attacked with foolish words, for it fuels him to look for a way to lash back at you.

The Book of Jude doesn't say Michael backed down, although I've heard it preached like that. We have been given the name of Jesus, and the authority behind that name, to cast out devils and to trample on every appearance of evil that raises its ugly head against God's Word. We have the authority to proclaim, "I rebuke you in the name of Jesus!" We have the authority and the commission from Jesus Christ to rebuke the devil, to rebuke sickness, to rebuke that tempter, or whatever else we are dealing with—but in every case, we speak and act in the name of Jesus. We are not to rail against a problem or get into the flesh.

Chapter 4

Exercise Your Authority With Humility and Boldness

It was June 5, 1988. The place was San Juan, Puerto Rico. Two months earlier the Lord had spoken to me about coming to this small Caribbean island to preach the Word of God. My finances were at the lowest point ever–I had $13 to my name. But I believed then, as I do now, that whatever the Lord orders, He pays for. I didn't tell anybody about my upcoming trip, but I prayed and sought the Lord. I made airline arrangements and waited for the Lord to do the rest.

Within a few short weeks I had received all the finances I needed, and I was given the name and phone number of some American Christians living in San Juan. They attended the only English-speaking church there, and it was through Gary and Kathy Adams that a door for ministry opened to me.

Every service was glorious, with many people coming to Christ and signs following. As we went out into the streets carrying a ten-foot cross and preaching, many people gave their lives to Jesus. We followed up with the people who received Christ by baptizing them in the Caribbean Sea.

One of the most astounding miracles took place when I visited a children's orphanage. An 18-month-old baby boy named Saul had been brought to the orphanage dying of AIDS. His mother was a drug addict, and she too was dying of the dreaded disease in a San Juan hospital. The doctor who was treating the little boy said he had only a short time to live. Saul's body was covered with sores. Even his mouth and throat were filled with white pussy sores, making it impossible for him to eat or swallow.

As I stood at the side of Saul's crib, the Holy Spirit prompted me to lay hands on him and pray for his healing. At that time I had not heard of anyone being healed of AIDS, but I believed what God's Word says in Mark 16:18: "They will lay hands on the sick, and they will recover." This promise is not limited to certain diseases; it means what it says. There were four other people with me, so we gathered around Saul's crib, laid hands on him, and prayed, believing God for the answer.

We continued our tour of the orphanage and spent some time with the other children there. After half an hour we went back to check on Saul. When we peered into his crib, it was obvious that his high fever had broken; his bed was totally soaked from perspiration. Saul had been listless for days, as he was always on the brink of death. But when he heard us, he clambered to his feet and greeted us with a big smile and a sparkle in his piercing blue eyes. The lady who operated the orphanage ran over and picked up little Saul to see if his fever had left. She peered into his mouth and began to rejoice—the pussy sores were gone! Then she gave Saul a bath and fed him his first meal in several days.

This lovely woman continued to praise God and tell us, "Baby Saul is healed! He is not going to die! He's healed!" I was reminded of the great excitement that filled the home of Jairus and his wife when their little girl was brought back to life. For days after that, I could hear the Lord speak to me, "Bill, did you see what I did for that little child? That's what I want to do. That is why Jesus died—to save, heal, and deliver." This miracle in Puerto Rico was possible because Jesus Christ gave me the authority of His name. Satan had to listen and obey my words just as he did when Jesus was on the earth healing the sick. Satan must obey your faith-filled words also, when he knows you believe what God's Word says.

The Rest of the Story

Four years later, the young man who had been with me when Saul was healed returned to Puerto Rico for a visit. He went back to the orphanage to ask how Saul was doing, and this is the report he was given:

Every Believer's Authority

The doctors confirmed Saul was healed and he became eligible for adoption after his mother died. His new family changed his name to Brian. This family had another son who was five or six years old, who had leukemia and wasn't expected to live very long. But after Brian (Saul) came to live with them, the son with leukemia was miraculously healed.

The father had been blind in one eye for many years. But after Brian (Saul) came to live with them, the father received his sight again miraculously! Praise and glory be to God!

The Lord still heals today! He wants to meet your every need. Psalm 37:4 says, "Delight yourself also in the Lord, and He shall give you the desires of your heart." The Book of Acts is still being written through those of God's people who will dare to believe all that Jesus taught.

Angels Are to Serve Us
The Book of Hebrews offers us a revealing view of the angelic activity that takes place behind the scenes of the tangible realm.

For to which of the angels did He ever say: "You are My Son, today I have begotten You"? And again: "I will be to Him a Father, and He shall be to Me a Son"? But when He again brings the firstborn into the world, He says: "Let all the angels of God worship Him." And of the angels He says: "Who makes His angels spirits and His ministers a flame of fire" (Hebrews 1:5-7).

God has made His angels spirits and His ministers a flame of fire. The angels are meant to serve us and work on our behalf to fulfill the purposes of God in the earth. The second part of verse 7 says, "and His ministers a flame of fire." The Greek word translated as "ministers" means *servants*. This term refers to those who follow Christ! It doesn't list "hellfire preachers" as "flames of fire"; it refers to all those who *serve the Lord* and follow Christ. God's Word says He makes His ministers a "flame of fire." Are you a servant of the Lord? Are you a flame of fire for the Lord?

The spirits are there to work with us, but it is we who have been given the Holy Spirit, not the angels. They are not filled with the Holy Ghost, or with the creative, declarative authority of the Father. They have the authority to help us, and they bear tidings of the Lord. However, we have the infilling of the Holy Spirit. The "fire" in this passage refers to the Holy Ghost and the authority contained in the vessels. We have the presence of the Holy Spirit with us.

"But to which of the angels has He ever said: 'Sit at My right hand, till I make Your enemies Your footstool'? Are they not all ministering spirits sent forth to minister for those who will inherit salvation?" (Heb. 1:13-14). Angels have been give to the saints who will inherit salvation. They are here to serve us. We can call on those angels; we can loose those angels; we can

Every Believer's Authority

send them on assignment to help us or to actually fight for us! That's right, the angels will go forth and fight a battle with demons to protect us and to keep us safe.

Follow the Word of God

Therefore we must give the more earnest heed to the things we have heard, lest we drift away. For if the word spoken through angels proved steadfast, and every transgression and disobedience received a just reward, how shall we escape if we neglect so great a salvation, which at the first began to be spoken by the Lord, and was confirmed to us by those who heard Him, God also bearing witness both with signs and wonders, with various miracles, and gifts of the Holy Spirit, according to His own will? (Hebrews 2:1-4)

If God has given this "great salvation" to us, and if He has given us this authority and told us what we are able to do, then how will we answer Him if we neglect it? If you have problems and situations in your life that continue to harass you because you don't operate in what God has done for you, what is He supposed to do? He has given you authority over demons. I realize that people have a free will, but you can pray and intercede for those people until those demons are defeated by the angels in Heaven. You can pray until those people want to get set free. Don't give up

60

Exercise Your Authority With Humility and Boldness

praying for your loved ones. We have a liberating gospel. Too many Christians quit before they get the answer. Jesus said He was sent to heal the brokenhearted and to "set at liberty" those who are held captive (Lk. 4:18 KJV). He has passed His commission to preach the gospel of the Kingdom to us and called us to pray.

We need to have more prayer, friends. You need to be interceding for your city and for the lost in your area. You need to get on your knees and cry out to God, and take authority over the demons in your area. If you do, you will see people set free! We are in a battle. We need to be in uniform and ready to march into combat.

Operate in the Authority Given to Us

Soteria is the Greek word translated in Hebrews 2:3 as "salvation." It means more than we think it does. We have been given healing. We have been given liberation. We have been given authority. If we neglect this salvation, what will we do about it? If we let our brothers and sisters go to hell and do nothing about it, how will we answer God? He has given a place, a position to operate in, and we need to operate in it. We need to use it. We need to take a stand against the evil forces on this earth and in the heavens. How shall we escape if we neglect so great a salvation? How shall we answer?

For He has not put the world to come, of which we speak, in subjection to angels, but one testified in a certain place, saying: "What is man

Every Believer's Authority

that You are mindful of him, or the son of man that You take care of him? You have made Him a little lower than the angels; You have crowned him with glory and honor, and set him over the works of Your hands. You have put all things in subjection under his feet" (Hebrews 2:5-8).

The world is not subject to the angels; it is subject to us! The Bible says, "What is man that You are mindful of him, or the son of man that You take care of him?" God has put us there with Christ. We have been put in charge with Him; the world is under us. Our authority is great on this earth, but we need to wake up and begin to exercise it!

The writer of Hebrews speaks of the sovereignty of Jesus Christ: "You have put all things in subjection under his feet" (Heb. 2:8a). Remember, we are ruling and reigning with Him, and according to Ephesians 2:6, we are seated in "heavenly places" with Him; so these things are under our feet.

We will trample on serpents and scorpions and all the works of the devil because God put them all in subjection under Jesus. Everything has been put under His nail-scarred feet.

For it was fitting for Him, for whom are all things and by whom are all things, in bringing many sons to glory, to make the captain of their salvation perfect through sufferings. For both He who sanctifies and those who are being sanctified are all of one, for which reason

He is not ashamed to call them brethren (Hebrews 2:10-11).

Doesn't that just bless you? You and Jesus Christ are seen as one. We are part of that family. The devil sees us as a brother of sister to Jesus and walking in His authority.

Stand Against the Devil With the Word of God

So, what are you going to do about it? It is up to you. You can allow satan to rule and reign and have his way simply by doing nothing. I am as guilty of that as anybody. There have been situations where I should have been in much greater prayer, and operated in much greater authority but didn't, and I had to repent. I am going to start checking things a whole lot closer, and you need to as well. If you have problems in your home, problems on the job, problems in your finances, or problems in your physical body, then you need to stand against the devil. Stand against his evil forces. Stand with the Word of God. Get the Word of God in you.

Bullet Removed Through the Power of God

In 1992, a man and his family visited our church during a Sunday service. At the end of the service, I took some time to pray for the sick, which I do at almost every service. This man came forward and asked for prayer for his left arm, since it was partially paralyzed. He was going to have to quit his job as a chef in a nice restaurant because he could no longer lift anything heavy.

Every Believer's Authority

He didn't tell me what the whole problem was, but as soon as I laid hands on him and prayed, he felt the power of God shoot through his body and total strength came back into his left arm. He began to cry, and then explained to me that he had been badly shot up in Vietnam 24 years earlier. During all those years, he had carried a sniper's bullet near his spine, which pinched nerves in his back. The problem was inoperable because of the bullet's position near the spinal cord. The doctors told him he would be in a wheelchair if the bullet moved. They also said that in a few years he would be totally paralyzed. But that day, for the first time since his injury, he could lift his arm!

The next Sunday he came back and gave us the rest of the story. He went to the doctors and had an X-ray taken of his back. To the astonishment of the doctors, the bullet in his spine was gone! They compared the new X-ray with previous X-rays that had showed the location of the bullet, but it wasn't to be found in the new X-ray. Glory be to God!

That man is still healed today. Those who believe still have the authority to heal the sick in the name of Jesus.

Exercise Your Authority With Humility and Boldness

There are three things that help us exercise the authority God has delegated to us. I realize that authority comes to us when we are born again, but I believe there are three things we must exercise in order for it to truly manifest and work. The first prerequisite is that we must *believe*.

Exercise Your Authority With Humility and Boldness

According to Ephesians 2:6, you and I are seated in heavenly places with Christ Jesus. You need to see yourself seated with Jesus beside the Father, with all the saints lined up. We are at the right hand of Jesus. Can you see the rows and rows of believers lined up so the authority passes from the Father to the Son to the saints? I have the same authority over satan that Jesus has. However, I need to believe that in order for it to work.

The second area or prerequisite that will help us exercise the authority God has delegated to us is *humility*. Peter doesn't leave any room for doubt: "God resists the proud, but gives grace to the humble" (1 Pet. 5:5b). God doesn't use proud people or braggarts. He uses people who are humble. "Therefore submit to God. Resist the devil and he will flee from you" (Jas. 4:7). Hallelujah! He will flee from you when you are humble.

Jesus said He did nothing but what the Father in Heaven showed Him (see Jn. 8:38). We must have that attitude too. We have to settle it in our hearts: "I am not going to do things unless God has really directed me to do them." All the power and authority that Jesus had on the earth was not of Himself—it was from the Father. We need to walk in that same humility. "The good things that are happening in my life are from God. I haven't done any good. If there is anything good in me at all, it is because of Christ Jesus. It is not that I am more educated than anybody; if anything good is happening, it is because God is helping

65

Every Believer's Authority

me. He helps the sinner. He rains upon the just and the unjust. He helps the unrighteous and blesses the righteous. He does good for both, desiring that all will come to salvation."

One of the danger zones arises when we put too much emphasis on material things "as a sign" that God truly loves us. We should never say, "That guy has a better car than me, so God must love him more." Nor should we ever say, "I have a better car than him, so God must love me more." No! Don't put any value on material things—always remember that the world will pass away. Praise God! When you see the authority of God operating in your life, when you see sickness go, when you see demons fleeing, when you see changed lives, then you know that the authority of God is operating in you.

First we need to believe that we have spiritual authority through Jesus Christ and the Holy Spirit abiding within. Then we need to be humble. Third, we need to have boldness. We need to walk in love, yet we need to be lion-hearted like the Lion of Judah. When it comes to the things that are dear to God, we must be ferocious and strong. Don't be a quitter. Don't give up. If something doesn't succeed, continue working at it with persistence. If you pray for somebody and you don't see results, don't quit. Pray longer and pray more. Pray until the sun comes up. Pray until you see that sickness go. Don't give in and don't give up!

Paul wrote, "Blessed be the God and Father of our Lord Jesus Christ, who has blessed us with every spiritual blessing in the heavenly places in Christ" (Eph. 1:3). You can have boldness because you have been blessed with every spiritual blessing in the heavenly places in Christ! We are blessed in the heavens; we are blessed on the earth. We are blessed and we can have boldness, so we need to have the belief. We need to have the humility and we need to have the boldness. We need to know that the things we say and the things we pray will come to pass. They will be answered.

Check these three areas in your life: Where does my belief lie? Where does my humility stand? Do I have boldness? Then ask yourself, "Will I willingly walk in this authority?" If you get these things straight in your life, then you will never have to fear man, spirit, or circumstance again! If you are not strong in every area, just start working on it. Just start making it happen. No matter what circumstance rises up, you will be able to deal with it. You will be able to speak to it and take authority over it. You won't have to be afraid of the demons. You won't have to be afraid of what man wants to do to you either. Just stand back and watch God work.

Take Authority Over Evil

Many times, I have seen the schemes of men fall away as I got close to God and took authority over the spirits that were controlling the schemers. I have seen people's mouths stop, and I've seen their actions immobilized by the hand of God. At times I almost felt bad for them because they were made to

Every Believer's Authority

look like fools when they planned evil. The Bible says the unrighteous will dig pits for the righteous and they will fall in it (Prov. 28:10). I have seen people fall deep into their pits while God protected me.

Don't get into the flesh. Don't get into your own thoughts. Don't be coming up with schemes: "Boy, am I going to fix this guy," or "Boy, I will just say this and do that." No sir! You just trust in God and speak the Word. Take authority over those demons and God will vindicate you and set you free. Praise God!

That is the way God wants us to live, in order that we will have no fear of man. After all, why should you fear man? What can he do to you? Hallelujah. What can the forces of the devil do to you if you exercise your authority? If you don't exercise it, though, they could take you over. But you have the power of deliverance in your mouth (Jesus). Praise God! Hallelujah. Praise the Lord!

And He said to them, "Go into all the world and preach the gospel to every creature. He who believes and is baptized will be saved; but he who does not believe will be condemned. And these signs will follow those who believe: In My name they will cast out demons; they will speak with new tongues; they will take up serpents; and if they drink anything deadly, it will by no means hurt them; they will lay hands on the sick, and they will recover." So then, after the Lord had spoken to them, He was received up into heaven, and sat down at the right hand

Exercise Your Authority With Humility and Boldness

of God. And they went out and preached everywhere, the Lord working with them and confirming the word through the accompanying signs. Amen (Mark 16:15-20).

Operate your life like this and miraculous confirmations, as verse 20 says, will happen. Only believe the Word and operate according to it.

Chapter 5

God's Word Gives Us Authority for Healing

Several years ago I learned that the mole on my right temple near my eye was a melanoma, a form of skin cancer. This thing was about the size of a dime, and when I learned it was cancer, my first reaction was to give into the paralyzing sting of fear. But then I remembered that Jesus was my Healer, just as He was the Healer who healed my son's ears, and who had performed many other healings I had seen and heard of.

I didn't spend a lot of time asking Jesus to heal me. Instead, I took the authority Jesus gave me in His name and used it to do battle with the cancer in my body. I rebuked the cancer and commanded it to dry up and leave in the name of Jesus Christ! Now I didn't have any confidence in my ability to heal anything or anybody, but I had a lot of confidence in my divine Physician. I laid my hand on that dark swollen sore as

Every Believer's Authority

I prayed, rebuked, and commanded according to God's unchanging Word. I never took any medicine or chemotherapy. I only took the Word of God.

After one week, I noticed that the mole had shrunk. I want you to note that *nothing happened immediately*, but I wasn't moved by what I saw. I was determined to be moved only by the Word of God and the Spirit of God working within me!

I thanked the Lord every day for healing me of cancer—even when I didn't see results—because I was believing the truth of God's Word. This is "standing on God's Word." According to Psalm 107:20, my Physician had "sent His word" to heal me, and I was going to take my medicine faithfully.

*Then they cried out to the Lord in their trouble, and He saved them out of their distresses. **He sent His word and healed them,** and delivered them from their destructions* (Psalm 107:19-20).

In Mark 11, the disciples were amazed that a fig tree had withered away in one day at Jesus' command. He answered them with these powerful words:

So Jesus answered and said to them, "Have faith in God. For assuredly, I say to you, whoever says to this mountain, 'Be removed and be cast into the sea,' and does not doubt in his heart, but believes that those things he says will be done, he will have whatever he says.

God's Word Gives Us Authority for Healing

Therefore I say unto you, whatever things you ask when you pray, believe that you receive them, and you will have them" (Mark 11:22-24).

When you speak to that mountain, don't doubt, only believe. For four weeks I spoke to that mountain of disease on my temple and watched as the cancerous bleeding mole continued to slowly shrink. It had to. It didn't have any choice. I had commanded it to do so in Jesus' name, and I didn't doubt. I believed the Word of God was true, and God's Word said healing was my inheritance in Jesus.

If I had doubted or questioned whether or not it was God's will to heal me, I would not have been healed. It is God's will to heal you. That's what His Word says. Don't let wrong teaching confuse you.

Who Himself bore our sins in His own body on the tree, that we, having died to sins, might live for righteousness—by whose stripes you were healed (1 Peter 2:24).

I was already healed by the stripes on Jesus' back, according to First Peter 2:24, so it was a "done deal." On the morning of the twenty-eighth day after the ordeal began, I looked in the mirror and discovered that the cancerous growth by my eye was totally gone—and it will never be back! I was healed by the Great Physician, Jesus Christ, and He wants to heal you today too. Believe His Word and act on it. Don't try to rationalize it or figure it out. Just believe it. My friend, God's Word still works the same way today.

Every Believer's Authority

Speak God's Word aloud over and over, and get it deep down inside you.

God's Word Gives Us Authority for Healing

In the previous chapters we looked at what God's Word says about the authority He has given every believer to trample on the power and servants of satan through Christ Jesus. Now we need to dig deeper into God's Word in the area of divine healing. Many today want to dispute what God's Word says on this subject because it is very "inconvenient" and "supernatural." Common sense and wisdom tell us the best way to understand a thing is to go to the source. It is about time for the Body of Christ to study God's Word and believe it—and I mean believe it more than man's ever-changing word!

My son, give attention to my words; incline your ear to my sayings. Do not let them depart from your eyes; keep them in the midst of your heart; for they are life to those who find them, and health to all their flesh (Proverbs 4:20-22).

The Word of God is clear and direct in its teachings about physical illness and divine healing: Healing operates through the spirit realm, not the natural. Healing ministers to your spirit. When your spirit receives healing from God, your body immediately responds as well and receives divine healing. God's desire is for us to continually walk and live in divine health through His Word, that we might totally fulfill God's purposes on the earth without hindrance.

God's Word Gives Us Authority for Healing

No, we don't have to establish a "new doctrine" about healing and physical and mental health. It has already been settled in Heaven that the Word of God is true, and that it heals. Jesus Christ Himself is our Healer today, and we don't have to have sickness in our bodies. We have the victory. If there is cancer in your body, if there is mental oppression or depression, if there is heart disease or any other foul thing that attacks the spirit man through the body, then you just don't have to put up with it! You don't have to receive it because Jesus has given you victory on the cross. He gave you the authority to deal with sickness and demons in His almighty name! He personally shed His precious blood to ransom your soul, and He forever purchased your healing by receiving the maximum 39 stripes from a cat-o'-nine-tails whip on His innocent back for you. Your healing is not a "maybe"; it is a "yea and amen" in God's eyes. Your access to Christ's healing flow is settled—forever.

Psalm 19:7 says, "The law of the Lord is perfect, converting the soul; the testimony of the Lord is sure, making wise the simple." The record is clear; the Word of the Lord is *perfect*. It is perfect and complete; it doesn't need anything added to it or taken away. It doesn't mean one thing one day and another thing the next. That may be the way men operate, but God isn't like men. He does not lie, change, or waver. When God says a thing, He means exactly what He says. God's Word is perfect, and you're not going to change it. It is the only thing on this earth that will

Every Believer's Authority

not change! Thus it is the eternal anchor God gave us to serve as a foundation for life and health.

Receive Your Healing by Faith

The first thing you should do if you aren't receiving your healing is to check your heart. Is there any unbelief there toward God's Word, or are there any doubts about the things of God? Are you walking in love toward everyone you know? One of the most important questions you and I can ask at any time and for any reason is this: "Is there unforgiveness in my heart toward anyone—someone who hurt me?"

So Jesus answered and said to them, "Have faith in God. For assuredly, I say to you, whoever says to this mountain, 'Be removed and be cast into the sea,' and does not doubt in his heart, but believes that those things he says will be done, he will have whatever he says. Therefore I say to you, whatever things you ask when you pray, believe that you receive them, and you will have them. And whenever you stand praying, if you have anything against anyone, forgive him, that your Father in heaven may also forgive you your trespasses. But if you do not forgive, neither will your Father in heaven forgive your trespasses" (Mark 11:22-26).

Verse 22 says the first step to receive healing is to "have faith in God." The Word of God and the God of the Word are the same. If someone says he has faith in

God's Word Gives Us Authority for Healing

God, but doesn't believe the Word, then in all honesty, he doesn't really have faith in God. You can't separate God from His Word. The possible limitation is mentioned by John, who said:

This is the disciple who testifies of these things, and wrote these things; and we know that his testimony is true. And there are also many other things that Jesus did, which if they were written one by one, I suppose that even the world itself could not contain the books that would be written. Amen (John 21:24-25).

Although the fullness of God is much greater and more glorious than even the written Word of God can contain, everything it does contain and relays to us is 100 percent God-breathed and anointed!

This Word is more than a collection of wise sayings or commandments; it is life and health and healing to us! Psalm 107:20 says, "He sent His word and healed them, and delivered them from their destructions." God sent His Word and healed us. Next we will look at faith and doubt through the doorway of God's eternal Word.

For assuredly, I say to you, whoever says to this mountain, "Be removed and be cast into the sea," and does not doubt in his heart, but believes that those things he says will be done, he will have whatever he says. Therefore I say unto you, whatever things you ask when you

Every Believer's Authority

pray, believe that you receive them, and you will have them (Mark 11:23-24).

When Jesus talked to the disciples about "moving a mountain," He wasn't talking about moving some large rock out of the way to get somewhere. He was talking about moving any kind of difficult situation or obstacle—such as sickness, lack, or demonic hindrance—that blocks your way to enjoying divine health and personal well-being, or fulfilling your God-given destiny or task. With Jesus, you have the authority to *command* that situation to leave your life and body. You have the authority in Christ Jesus to command that demonic obstacle to be thrown into the sea so you can pass into God's promised land and purposes according to His will! If you don't *doubt* in your heart, but believe, it will be done.

Mark 11:24 tells us to believe even before we receive! Don't believe the scoffers. This isn't some "off the wall" teaching concocted by some fanatic who has purposely twisted the Word for his own profit. These are the words of the *Incarnate Son of God* Himself who purchased our freedom from sin and death with His life, and took 39 stripes on His back to win our freedom from sickness and disease! He came that we might have "abundant" life in His grace! (See John 10:10.) According to Jesus Christ, faith is "believing something before it happens."

Many Christians today are faithfully following in the footsteps of Thomas. He is the disciple famous for managing to spend three world-shaking years literally

God's Word Gives Us Authority for Healing

within touching distance of Jesus Christ, and emerging with no more faith than he had before he met Him! Millions of Bible students know this man as "Doubting Thomas" because he operated in such doubt and unbelief that he almost dismissed the greatest miracle of all time, the miraculous resurrection of the Messiah, Jesus Christ, three days after His death and burial.

Millions of people are missing the truth and power of God's Word today. They are missing out on their miracles and healings because they won't put their faith in Jesus Christ and His Word! They can trust Him with the greater miracle of saving their souls, but they refuse to trust His Word enough to receive the divine healing He promised. It is like saying, "I don't mind jumping in the lake, but I don't believe in getting wet—now that's just too far out." Are you a Thomas? You can be a man or woman of faith.

And whenever you stand praying, if you have anything against anyone, forgive him, that your Father in heaven may also forgive you your trespasses. But if you do not forgive, neither will your Father in heaven forgive your trespasses (Mark 11:25-26).

The most common reason our prayers are not answered (including our prayers for healing), is that we have not forgiven others. God cannot bless or reward unforgiveness. Everything He did for us through His Son is based on forgiveness, mercy, and grace. Jesus said we must forgive others if we are going to be for-given, yet many Christians continue to harbor unfor-giveness toward their wives or husbands, toward their parents or their children, and toward others who have hurt them. This hinders them from receiv-ing what God wants to do in their lives.

At one time in my ministry, I counseled a lady who had been sexually molested as a teenager. That is a terrible thing to have happen to you at any age. It causes guilt and despair, and it has ruined many a per-son's life. When I talked to this lady about her need to forgive the individual who abused her, she said she had forgiven him, but it wasn't true because the issue kept coming up.

Her terrible experience, and the unforgiveness she would not release, caused her unbearable mental an-guish and torment. Finally, her inner torment led to mental illness. After a while, she stopped coming for counseling. Because she refused to let go of the past and forgive, her condition quickly got worse. She be-came more depressed and mentally unbalanced, when the truth was she didn't have to. Her path to wholeness would not have been easy by any means, but God's grace would have been sufficient for her need if she would have received it.

The passage in Isaiah 53:5 says the Messiah, Jesus Christ, was the chastisement for our peace. He paid the price to heal everyone of mental and physical ill-ness. Our mental hospitals are full today because peo-ple have not forgiven others and allowed Jesus Christ

God's Word Gives Us Authority for Healing

to heal them. Check your heart right now. If there is anything in it that is not pure, lovely, and good, then give it to Jesus. He paid the price for your healing and deliverance. Get set free and receive the answer to your prayers. Believe and receive your healing.

The Gospel of Mark records one of the most remarkable healings in the New Testament: the healing of the "woman with the issue of blood." This miracle is remarkable because it reveals the role of persistent faith in the healing process of God.

And there was a woman who had had a flow of blood for twelve years, and who had endured much suffering under [the hands of] many physicians and had spent all that she had, and was no better but instead grew worse. She had heard the reports concerning Jesus, and she came up behind Him in the throng and touched His garment, for she kept saying, If I only touch His garments, I shall be restored to health (Mark 5:25-28 AMP).

Can't you just see this frail, sickly woman in the middle of that jostling, tightly packed crowd? The whole time, her entire being was focused on only one goal: *If I can just touch His garment*! "If I can just touch His garment, I will be healed! If I can just touch His garment, I will be healed! If I can just touch His garment, I will be healed!" Praise God!

That destitute, desperate woman started to build the faith up in her heart. She started to repeat the

Every Believer's Authority

truth she had heard. She "had heard the reports concerning Jesus." She had heard the good word. She heard what He could do. She was repeating over and over what she had heard about her Healer. She just kept going through these words and building up her faith, and it excited her spirit and energized her drained and afflicted body. "If I can just touch His garment, I will be healed! If I can just touch the hem of His garment, I will be healed!" Then she went to the One with all authority.

This woman was so energized by the Word that she waded into a crowd that was so tightly packed that some scholars feel it was suffocating. She could easily have lost her life in that dangerous situation, but she was on a mission inspired by God's Word. She had nothing to lose and everything to gain. She put her total unconditional faith in God, and in this mysterious Man who had the power to heal! When she somehow managed to touch Jesus' garment, the Word says that instantly her "flow of blood" dried up and she was healed. Glory to God! She never even asked permission of Jesus to be healed. She simply took authority by believing the Word she had heard about Jesus.

She had heard the reports concerning Jesus, and she came up behind Him in the throng and touched His garment, for she kept saying, If I only touch His garments, I shall be restored to health. And immediately her flow of blood was dried up at the source, and [suddenly] she

God's Word Gives Us Authority for Healing

felt in her body that she was healed of her [distressing] ailment. And Jesus, recognizing in Himself that the power proceeding from Him had gone forth, turned around immediately in the crowd and said, Who touched My clothes? And the disciples kept saying to Him, You see the crowd pressing hard around You from all sides, and You ask, Who touched Me? (Mark 5:27-31 AMP)

When Jesus asked, "Who touched Me?" His disciples, being the astute men that they were, said, "Well, Lord, look at all the people around You. What do You mean, who touched You? Everybody is touching You." But Jesus didn't drop the matter there. He basically told them, "There is somebody here with faith. There is somebody here who believes in Me. There is somebody here who has drawn virtue from Me. Who is it?"

Still He kept looking around to see her who had done it. But the woman, knowing what had been done for her, though alarmed and frightened and trembling, fell down before Him and told Him the whole truth. And He said to her, Daughter, your faith (your trust and confidence in Me, springing from faith in God) has restored you to health. Go in (into) peace and be continually healed and freed from your [distressing bodily] disease (Mark 5:32-36 AMP).

Every Believer's Authority

That little woman meekly confessed, "It's me," and bowed down at the Lord's feet. But she misunderstood the Lord's intentions. He wasn't upset over her aggressive pursuit of healing—He wanted His disciples, and those who would follow later, to learn from her aggressive, persistent faith! Jesus said, "Your faith has made you well." Praise God! Hallelujah. This woman believed the Word. It was medicine to her sickness. Her faith allowed her to apply the Word she had heard about God to her sickness. She had faith to believe and she received a divine cure for her sickness—and Jesus made her a landmark of faith and inspiration for countless generations to follow!

Chapter 6

Don't Put God in a Box

The Book of Second Kings provides one of the countless proofs that God's Word works the same in any generation, situation, culture, or setting. The record of Naaman's divinely orchestrated encounter with the prophet Elisha provides some valuable lessons for us as we seek divine health in our day. Then, as now, it all hinged on the Word of God.

Now Naaman, commander of the army of the king of Syria, was a great and honorable man in the eyes of his master, because by him the Lord had given victory to Syria. He was also a mighty man of valor, but a leper. And the Syrians had gone out on raids, and had brought back captive a young girl from the land of Israel. She waited on Naaman's wife. Then she said to her mistress, "If only my master were with the prophet who is in Samaria! For he would heal him of his leprosy." And Naaman went in and told his master, saying, "Thus

Every Believer's Authority

and thus said the girl who is from the land of Israel. Then the king of Syria said, "Go now, and I will send a letter to the king of Israel." So he departed and took with him ten talents of silver, six thousand shekels of gold, and ten changes of clothing. Then he brought the letter to the king of Israel, which said, Now be advised, when this letter comes to you, that I have sent Naaman my servant to you, that you may heal him of his leprosy (2 Kings 5:1-6).

The last verse in the passage above reveals a misunderstanding on the part of this Syrian king. Whether it was because he was working with a third-hand news source, or because he figured the prophet had to be under the employ and total command of the king of Israel, he wrote to the king rather than to the prophet.

And it happened, when the king of Israel read the letter, that he tore his clothes and said, "Am I God, to kill and make alive, that this man sends a man to me to heal him of his leprosy? Therefore please consider, and see how he seeks a quarrel with me." So it was, when Elisha the man of God heard that the king of Israel had torn his clothes, that he sent to the king, saying, "Why have you torn your clothes? Please let him come to me, and he shall know that there is a prophet in Israel." Then Naaman went with his horses and chariot, and he stood at the door of Elisha's house. And

Don't Put God in a Box

Elisha sent a messenger to him, saying, "Go and wash in the Jordan seven times, and your flesh shall be restored to you, and you shall be clean" (2 Kings 5:7-10).

Elisha did not come out of his house, nor did he invite the leper inside. Why? Was he afraid of leprosy? No. Elisha was under the command of the Lord. He wanted to be careful not to appear to be the healer of Naaman. If Naaman focused his faith and hopes on Elisha and looked to him as the source of his healing, he wouldn't get healed. It wasn't the prophet who was the healer; only the almighty God could heal this man's disease!

Naaman was a senior general or commander in the powerful Syrian military machine. He was a mighty man of valor. He was tall and handsome; he had a nice suntan, wore all the right clothes, had the latest haircut, and hung around only with the finest of people—despite his affliction. Elisha the prophet wasn't like that. He didn't care what his hair looked like. He wasn't too concerned about the style of fashion. In the natural, when Naaman would see him, he would look at him and say, "Who is this guy? He is worse off than I am. I might be a leper, but look at him."

People look at the outward appearance and do things according to their own outward judgment. Elisha operated under God's authority as His mouthpiece. That is why he stayed in the house where it was dark and didn't show himself. What did he do? He spoke the Word of the Lord, not the word of a man. He gave a command that just didn't make a lot

Every Believer's Authority

of sense to the human mind. He told this well-dressed and incredibly powerful general who commanded the most powerful army in the region: "Go and wash in the Jordan seven times and you will be clean."

> *But Naaman became furious, and went away and said, "Indeed, I said to myself, 'He will surely come out to me, and stand and call on the name of the Lord his God, and wave his hand over the place, and heal the leprosy'"* (2 Kings 5:11).

On his way to see the great prophet in Israel, Naaman had said to himself, "Yeah, this is the way it will probably be...." He had preconceived ideas about his healing, and it just didn't happen the way he figured it would. Sounds like religion, doesn't it? "Well, this is the way we have always done it, so this is the way it has to be. Yeah, I have an idea that guy will just come out in some really bright robes and say, 'You're healed! You're healed! You're healed!'" Naaman had his own agenda and vision of what should be, but he found out the hard way that that wasn't the plan of God.

When Naaman didn't get his healing the way he wanted it and when he wanted it, he started to rationalize things in his mind. That is the worst thing you can do when you are reading the Word of God. You are in deep trouble anytime you start asking, "Why doesn't God do it my way?" Naaman refused to accept the Word of God. Instead, He said, "Are not the Abanah and the Pharpar, the rivers of Damascus, better than all the waters of Israel? Could I not wash in them and be clean?" The Bible tells us he actually "turned and went away in a rage." (See Second Kings 5:12.)

His limited finite mind rationalized that his healing had something to do with the purity of the water. If that was the problem, then he would have been right: the Jordan was a muddy river that wasn't very attractive. He figured that the dirty water of the Jordan River would just make him worse! He was thinking that the rivers in his own country were much cleaner.

The problem is that reasoning and rationalizing can only take you so far. He wasn't looking at the Word of God, which was the only thing that could give his healing. Naaman was confusing the agent of God's healing with the God who heals. No human vessel or agent is "clean enough" in their own right to bring blessing, healing, or salvation to any man. We are all muddy rivers. But we shouldn't be looking at the river—we need to look at the Word that empowers the river waters!

The Word of God to Naaman was to do a certain thing in a certain place and he would be healed. He was given the coordinates and the conditions of his appointment with the divine Healer. The Word of God tells us today to believe God's Word and receive God's blessings. Everything, you see, is rooted and motivated by God's Spirit.

Naaman was in the natural. He was still operating in his head knowledge, in his ideas. It had to happen that way. Wasn't he a mighty general who was recognized far and wide for his wisdom and military ability?

Every Believer's Authority

Did he look like a fool who would willingly embarrass himself by bathing in a filthy foreign river? If this Israelite God couldn't minister to him in the way he figured he deserved, well, it wasn't going to be. That, my friend, is "putting God in a box." Listen, telling God how He should do things will not bring results from His Word!

Then something interesting happened in verse 13: "And his servants came near and spoke to him..." (2 Kings 5:13). What does the Bible call the Holy Spirit? It calls Him our Helper. Naaman's anger could have earned him a lifelong dose of leprosy, but his servants spoke to him and turned him around. If you get off in wrong thinking, hopefully your spirit, being led of the Holy Spirit, will urge you to do the right thing. The Holy Spirit is always gentle. If you get off base and begin to think wrong things about God's Word or entertain preconceived ideas, the Holy Spirit will softly say to you, "Why are you acting like this? Why are you doing this? Have you forgotten what My Word says?" The wise response is, "Lord, I will get back on track."

Naaman's servants came to him "...and said, 'My father, if the prophet had told you to do something great, would you not have done it? How much more then, when he says to you, "Wash, and be clean"?' " (2 Kings 5:13). Naaman took the correction. He made the adjustment.

So he went down and dipped seven times in the Jordan, according to the saying of the man of God; and his flesh was restored like the flesh

90

of a little child, and he was clean. And he returned to the man of God, he and all his aides, and came and stood before him; and he said, "Indeed, now I know that there is no God in all the earth, except in Israel; now therefore, please take a gift from your servant" (2 Kings 5:14-15).

Naaman swallowed his pride, took a bath in the dirty Jordan River, and then he traveled 30 miles back, a two-day journey, just to see Elisha. This time Elisha came out of the house and stood before him. Now it didn't make any difference what Naaman saw or what Elisha's appearance was. Why? The man, Naaman, had acted upon the Word of God. We need to act upon God's Word too, so we can be healed and set free of the things that hinder us.

In Luke 4:27, Jesus refers to Naaman and his deliverance from leprosy. The Lord had just launched His public ministry by reading the Messianic passage from the scroll of Isaiah, and declared that He was the fulfillment of Isaiah's prophecy. It was here that He publicly proclaimed that He had been sent to heal the sick and to open blind eyes (see Lk. 4:18-21). Immediately the Pharisees challenged and questioned Him. They didn't have any faith in what He was doing, and Jesus told them, "...no prophet is accepted in his own country" (Lk. 4:24).

Jesus then told the people in the synagogue that in the time of Elijah, during the famine, there was only one woman—a foreign widow—who was sustained by the prophet of God, although there were many needy

Every Believer's Authority

widows in Israel. In Naaman's time, many Jews in Israel had leprosy, but God chose to heal a Syrian general. Why was only Naaman healed? Jesus brought up these controversial healings to rebuke the hypocritical Pharisees for doubting and refusing to believe that Jesus was the Messiah foretold in the ancient Scriptures.

Why weren't the needy widows and lepers in Israel helped during those times? They were not acting upon the Word of God. They were not operating in faith that God could heal them, or meet their needs during a time of drought. They had all heard of the prophets Elijah and Elisha. They had heard about the power of God, but they kept their eyes and faith on the circumstances. They looked at the drought and had great faith that it would continue. They looked at the withered trees and their faith in their calamity caused them to forgot about God. The people suffering from leprosy looked at the terrible disease destroying their bodies and they forgot how great God was and what He had done in the past. Only the foreigner, the outsider named Naaman, believed the reports, and even he nearly managed to let his faith in his disease and his preconceptions about God rob him of his healing. We almost didn't get to read about Naaman's miraculous healing. If it hadn't been for his servants who gave him a godly perspective, he would have been a nameless part of the forgotten past.

Naaman is a picture of the modern man who enters the scene with all kinds of money, loaded with all kinds of silver and gold. He was going to buy his healing, and he knew just how the scene should work.

The only problem was that God wasn't for sale. Elisha wasn't going to take the man's money or treasures. God's blessing was a free gift back then, and it is a free gift today. Only simple faith in God's Word will heal you. The authority of God's Word overcomes every disease and sickness still today.

One of the biggest objections made to divine healing today is based on the passage in Second Corinthians 12 about Paul's "thorn in the flesh." The argument usually goes something like this: "What about Paul? He had a thorn in the flesh. He was sick. God didn't heal him. He even asked God three times for healing, but He didn't heal him. Paul was a mighty man of God. He wrote most of the New Testament, and he was sick and God refused to heal him." Have you ever heard this?

I think this question deserves some serious consideration. What was Paul actually suffering with? What was this thorn in his flesh?

It is doubtless not profitable for me to boast. I will come to visions and revelations of the Lord: I know a man in Christ who fourteen years ago—whether in the body I do not know, or whether out of the body I do not know, God knows—such a one was caught up to the third heaven. And I know such a man—whether in the body or out of the body I do not know, God knows—how he was caught up into Paradise and heard inexpressible words, which it is not lawful for a man to utter. Of such a one I will

Every Believer's Authority

boast; yet of myself I will not boast, except in my infirmities (2 Corinthians 12:1-5)

Paul is talking about some out-of-body experiences. He got caught up in the Spirit of God and was taken into the third heaven. Paul was brought into the presence of God. He saw and heard things that he couldn't utter or repeat. He couldn't find words to describe or explain his incredible experience.

The apostle goes on to describe his "infirmities" in this passage, and the Amplified Bible offers a particularly clear understanding of Paul's words:

Of this same [man's experiences] I will boast, but of myself [personally] I will not boast, except as regards my infirmities (my weaknesses). Should I desire to boast, I shall not be a witless braggart, for I shall be speaking the truth. But I abstain [from it], so that no one may form a higher estimate of me than [is justified by] what he sees in me or hears from me. And to keep me from being puffed up and too much elated by the exceeding greatness (preeminence) of these revelations, there was given me a thorn (a splinter) in the flesh, a messenger of Satan, to rack and buffet and harass me, to keep me from being excessively exalted. Three times I called upon the Lord and besought [Him] about this and begged that it might depart from me; but He said to me, My grace (My favor and loving-kindness and mercy) is enough for you [sufficient against any danger and enables you to bear the trouble manfully]; for My strength and power are made perfect (fulfilled and completed) and show themselves most effective in [your] weakness. Therefore, I will all the more gladly glory in my weaknesses and infirmities, that the strength and power of Christ (the Messiah) may rest (yes, may pitch a tent over and dwell) upon me! (2 Corinthians 12:5-9 AMP)

For the word translated "infirmities" in verse 5, Paul used the Greek word, *astheneia*, which means weakness, not sickness. Paul was boasting in his weakness, not in a physical sickness. The Word says that God takes the foolish things of the world and uses them to confound the wise (see 1 Cor. 1:27). Paul sees himself as one of the least likely men to be chosen by God for the ministry. He believed there was nothing about him that would enable him to preach the gospel, yet God chose to use him, and he didn't know why.

I have felt that way. "Why would God use somebody like me? There are so many people that are better educated and better qualified. They do everything better. Why would God choose me?" The truth is that God chooses us, complete with our infirmities, our weaknesses, and our pasts. The word *infirmity* does not mean sickness. Do you have weaknesses in your character or personality? Maybe you have a hot temper. Maybe you lie once in a while and you shouldn't.

Maybe you have ungodly thoughts. As a Christian, you look at these things and say, "Oh Lord, these things should not be," and yet God uses you in your weaknesses. This is what Paul is talking about in Second Corinthians 12.

Go back to Second Corinthians 11:30 (AMP): "If I must boast, I will boast of the things that [show] my infirmity [of the things by which I am made weak and contemptible in the eyes of my opponents]." How about that? Paul is not talking about sickness. He is talking about his opponents. There were people who followed Paul around and slandered him. He would go into a place and raise up a group of people, lead them to the Lord, cast out devils, heal the sick, and start churches. But as soon as he would leave town, those wolves would come in and pervert the gospel. They would run down Paul and say things about him that weren't true. You can read about it in the letters to the Galatians and the Corinthians. He constantly corrected these problems and countered these lies. He had some hateful, dedicated opponents. So here he is talking about some of these things that his opponents were doing to cause him trouble.

It has been said that Paul was a man of short stature and that he wasn't very handsome. He didn't have a real pleasant appearance, and some even say he had a high, squeaky voice. Whatever the case was, there were things in his character and appearance that his opponents used against him. These things became such a thorn in his flesh that Paul asked God to remove them.

Don't Put God in a Box

In verse 9, Paul described the Lord's reply to his request for deliverance from the "thorn": "But He said to me, My grace (My favor and loving-kindness and mercy) is enough for you [sufficient against any danger and enables you to bear the trouble manfully]" (2 Cor. 12:9a AMP). This passage doesn't say anything about sickness. It says no matter what problems you have, be a man because of God's grace.

There were Christians in that day who knew about Paul and who probably said, "That dirty scoundrel. He arrested hundreds of people. Back in Jerusalem, he had them thrown into prison, and some of them were even executed! Now this man dares to call himself a Christian and a servant of Christ. How can you people follow after him?" That was a thorn in his flesh.

The Lord says, "Stand up. Stand up. This thing isn't going to leave you, but don't even worry about it. What is the big deal? Aren't I with you? Isn't My grace sufficient for you? Isn't My strength, My boldness, My life, and everything I have poured out to My Son, Jesus Christ, on the cross enough for you? Be a man (or woman). Stand up to the opposition. Stand up to your opponents. Don't you be moved by what anybody says about you. I have given you My authority to preach the gospel, heal the sick, and cast out devils. So do it."

Like Paul, we need to get to the point where we are not moved by what people think about us. If someone goes behind your back and wreaks havoc in your church or job, that is not your concern. Just do

Every Believer's Authority

what you are supposed to do and God will take care of the rest of the mess. I am not going to say that my interpretation of Paul's "thorn" is gospel, but this is the way I understand it, according to these Scriptures. I'm confident about it because Paul even used the word "harassment" to describe this "thorn."

He writes, "...there was given me a thorn (a splinter) in the flesh, a messenger of Satan, to rack and buffet and harass me..." (2 Cor. 12:7 AMP). What is harassment? It is a mental attack or taunting thoughts, but it is not sickness. He never mentions sickness. God's answer was simple and conclusive: "My grace will cover you." Be a man. Praise God!!

So the next time somebody says to you, "What about Paul? He had a thorn in his flesh, didn't he?" You just agree with them. "Yes, Paul had a 'thorn,' but it was just a lie of the devil that was out to destroy or at least hinder him." The enemy was trying to keep Paul from speaking out about Jesus with boldness. God gave him the boldness that he needed to continue on—it never had anything to do with sickness. The "thorn" never had anything to do with Paul's eyes; it had to do with the devil harassing him. This is one of satan's tactics to stop God's servant from operating in the authority that comes from Jesus Christ. Satan tries to discourage us.

If you have a thorn in the flesh, it won't harm you because God is greater than any evil thing the devil has. No matter what the adversary raises up and throws at you, as long as you go on with God and

Don't Put God in a Box

serve and love Him, His grace will be sufficient for you! Hallelujah!

Don't let any thorn in the flesh be a "monkey wrench" in the engine of your belief. God wants to heal you, and God wants you to be in health. He has a lot of work for you to do. Jesus has already paid the price for your healing. He has given you authority over sickness. Now it is up to you to stand up in the power of His might and do battle.

The Word of God says in Psalm 107:20, "He sent His word and healed them, and delivered them from their destructions." He sent His Word. He sent His Word in the beginning. "In the beginning was the Word" and "the Word became flesh and dwelt among us" (Jn. 1:1,14). Hallelujah! The Word is what set us free.

The next time sickness comes upon you or tries to come upon you, don't say, "Well, it must be God's will." Don't be like the Hindus who say, "Oh, did I do something wrong in a previous life? Is this God's punishment for me?" If you are born again, then you are the righteousness of God through Christ Jesus (see 2 Cor. 5:21). God doesn't use sickness to harass you or wreak havoc on you. He doesn't "give you" cancer to humble you or bring you to repentance. Your lack of humility, a sin, or your pride may throw you into the hands of the devil—and he will gladly give you something like that, but not God! When you repent and get right with God, you will get what God has for you again. Isn't that glorious?

Every Believer's Authority

Look at this powerful promise from the Book of Romans: "But if the Spirit of Him who raised Jesus from the dead dwells in you, He who raised Christ from the dead will also give life to your mortal bodies through His Spirit who dwells in you" (Rom. 8:11). We dwell in mortal bodies. God says He will give life to us. The same Spirit of God who raised Jesus from the dead *also* dwells in us if we are born again.

If the Spirit of God dwells in you, He will bring life into you. He will also bring healing to you! It is a settled subject. You don't have to question it or ask about it. Don't ever ask God, "God, is it Your will to heal me?" Instead say, "God, I thank You that it is Your will to heal me. I thank You that Your Word has spelled it out. I thank You for the promises." It doesn't say He will heal you if He feels like it. It says He has already healed you!

Peter the apostle wrote, "by whose stripes you were healed" (1 Pet. 2:24). By His stripes I am healed. By His stripes, I will not get sick. Glory to God! I don't believe in heart conditions, or arterial sclerosis. I don't believe in diabetes, liver problems, or brain tumors either. I don't even believe in ingrown toenails! I just don't receive them. I just repeat the Word. I repeat God's unchanging Word like the woman with the issue of blood did. You need to speak it too. Speak it aloud and speak it over your body and over your life. Speak God's Word over your wife, speak it over your husband, speak it over your children. If you have to, write it down on a piece of paper and keep it

100

Don't Put God in a Box

in your pocket so you can read it. Read it, speak it, believe it, and let it get down into your spirit.

God is not a God of confusion. He is not a fickle God who decides one thing today and something else tomorrow. He is not playing with your life; He has your life on a straight track like a locomotive. He has you barreling down that track, and He hasn't thrown pilings on the it just to see how you will jump across it. There are other things out there that are trying to derail you, but not God.

When evening had come, they brought to Him many who were demon-possessed. And He cast out the spirits with a word, and healed all who were sick, that it might be fulfilled which was spoken by Isaiah the prophet, saying: "He Himself took our infirmities and bore our sicknesses" (Matthew 8:16-17).

Jesus Christ has already borne your sickness. He is not giving it to you—He has already taken it from you! Take authority over it and command it to go in Jesus' name! Operate in the authority of Jesus Christ!

I hope you have enjoyed *Every Believer's Authority*. The purpose in writing this book was so every believer could reach his or her full potential in Christ Jesus and bring glory to God.

If you would like to receive more information about Living Faith Ministries or a complete list of other books and tapes available, or if you would like to arrange a time of ministry in your church or conference, please write:

Bill Ferg
c/o Living Faith Ministries
P.O. Box 791
Ashland, WI 54806

Books by Bill Ferg

B-101 Every Believer's Authority
Last days teaching on our authority over Satan, sickness, disease, and poverty, all in the mighty name of Jesus. $6.99

B-102 Job Was not God's Pawn
What really happened to Job? Why did he suffer? This book will explain it. $3.99

B-103 He Sent His Word to Heal You
You can receive your healing. Healing is yours because Jesus paid the price for your sin and sickness. This book will be a great encouragement to you. $6.50

Qty.	Book	Price	Total
	B-101 Every Believer's Authority	$6.99	
	B-102 Job Was not God's Pawn	$3.99	
	B-103 He Sent His Word to Heal You	$6.50	
	Subtotal		
	Postage and Handling (See chart below)		
	TOTAL		

Postage and Handling

$10.00 or less	$2.00
$10.01–$25.00	$3.00
$25.01–$50.00	$4.00
$50.00 or more (U.S.)	add 10%
$50.00 or more (Canada)	add 35%

NAME _____

ADDRESS _____

CITY _____

STATE _____ ZIP _____

Thank you for your order. Mail order to:

**Living Faith Ministries
P.O. Box 791
Ashland, WI 54806**

WISDOM POWER
by Kenneth Edlin.
Do you want more of God's wisdom, knowledge, and power in your life? Are you looking for inner happiness and mental freedom? God has a strategy to help you find these things! In *Wisdom Power* you'll learn God's method for transforming your thought life and becoming a successful citizen of the Kingdom.
TPB-196p.
ISBN 1-56043-832-0
Retail $7.99

To order toll free call:
Destiny Image
1-800-722-6774

THE ENLIGHTENED CHURCH: SATAN WHO?
by Dr. Karl A. Barden.
Too many Christians live in fear and intimidation of what the enemy may do to them next. That can all change when believers understand their proper authority over him. In this book Dr. Barden unveils the revelation of the correct way to view satan—defeated at the cross!
TPB-224p.
ISBN 1-56043-135-0
Retail $8.99

To order toll free call:
Destiny Image
1-800-722-6774